The *Parents*™ Baby and Childcare Series combines the most up-to-date medical findings, the advice of doctors and child psychologists, and the actual day-to-day experiences of parents like you. Covering a wide variety of subjects, these books answer all your questions, step-by-important-step, and provide the confidence of knowing you're doing the best for your child—with help from *Parents*™ Magazine.

Other *Parents*™ Childcare Books
*Published by Ballantine Books:*

# Parents™
## Book of
# Baby
# Names

## MARTIN KELLY

BALLANTINE BOOKS • NEW YORK

Library of Congress Catalog Card Number: 85-90715

ISBN 0-345-31428-X

Manufactured in the United States of America

First Edition: September 1985
Tenth Printing: February 1989

Cover Photograph by Mariano Pastor

# Contents

# The Choosing of the Name

We wanted a name, not too fancy or plain;
More common than Unagh, less common than Jane.
 Francesca was different, yet not too bizarre.
 It conjured up sea wind and moon and guitar.
Still it was earthy and gallant and strong.
Quite perfect in length; not too short, not too long.
 So I called to report to my Brooklyn aunt.
 When I mentioned the name, she said, "But you
  can't!"
"You don't like Francesca?" I said. "What a shame.
Of all names for girls, it's our favorite name."
 "I adore it," she said. "It charms and delights.
 But Francesca is sweeping through Brooklyn Heights!
There are six on my block and one right upstairs.
There are days when one sees them strolling in pairs.
 My Herbie has one in his piccolo class.
 Flo says there are two in percussion and brass."
So once more we sloshed through puddles of names,
More common than Cuthbert, less common than James.
 We bumbled through names by the bushel, the peck;
 Names à la Russe, à l'Anglaise, à la Grecque.
We listed close relatives here and abroad:
Fabrizio, Vyacheslav, Shrulnik and Maud.
 He thought of his kinfolk outside Milano:
 Aunt Fortunata and Uncle Arcano.

I remembered some cousins in Leningrad:
One Stanislav (Stanley?), one Vladimir (Vlad?).
> He remembered a distant cousin, Lavinia,
> Who mailed him prosciutto first-class from
> Sardinia.

One night in his dreams, he moaned, "Grandpa Dante
Lived till he died in Delicto Flagrante!"
> Then he woke up and said, "I cannot sleep nights
> 'Cause Francesca is sweeping through Brooklyn
> Heights.

Who cares if it's common as ailanthus trees,
Peanuts' mementos or children's skinned knees?
> Francesca, Francesca—the name's a delight.
> Tell Auntie from Brooklyn to go fly a kite."

The dilemma resolved, it seems fair to tell
That when she arrived, she was named Gabrielle.

*Charlotte Pomerantz*

# Introduction

Whenever I asked parents what they'd like to see in a book about names, the response was almost always the same: "Lots of names, with more information than the other books."

This was a logical answer, but I soon realized that it posed a dilemma. The more names you have, the less room there is for information about them; on the other hand, the more information you include, the less possibility there is to add more names.

I've tried to solve the problem by taking two different approaches. In chapters 8 and 9, you'll find a selective list of names for girls and boys, intended to achieve a balance between old favorites and more recent popular additions and variations. Obviously, the process of selection has been personal to some extent, but I've also been guided by the results of my own survey of parents' preferences, described in chapter 3. By being selective, we're able to give you more highlights on the path followed by a name from its origin down to the present day.

The index provides a more extensive list, including many other names that may be of interest to you, together with their derivations and meanings. In addition, the opening chapters offer some hints on the art of choosing a name, with examples to assist you.

I hope this combination meets the needs expressed by parents, and that it will help you find the perfect name for your one-of-a-kind baby.

# 1. Your Baby's Name: The Gift That Lasts a Lifetime

If you are like most expectant couples, one of the first things you learn about selecting a name for your baby is that there's more to it than you thought. Generally, parents approach the task of naming with a kind of relaxed anticipation: it all seems so simple ahead of time. But unless they have definitely made up their minds in advance—and few have—they soon find that the process of naming is much more complex than they assumed.

This is a fairly recent phenomenon. In the past there were limitations to the possibility of naming—official restrictions that still exist today in some countries. Throughout much of our history, one basis for these limitations was religious. The Hebrew people were expected to choose names that embodied their heritage; the early Christians developed a long list of martyrs' names that were passed on from one generation to the next. After the Protestant Reformation, any name that did not appear in the Bible or personify a virtue was regarded by the Puritans and other groups as idolatrous. When the Pilgrims arrived in America, they brought with them this strong emphasis on biblical names and names of virtues.

Later arrivals in the United States introduced—as they still do—a diversity of religious, national, and ethnic backgrounds, each with its own traditions. Some families sought to perpetuate these traditions, while others wanted to become "American" as quickly as possible. One way of doing that was to select names for their children from among those of famous figures of their adopted country—Washington, Jefferson, Jackson, Lincoln, and others.

Family history has also been a source of limitation on name selection. If a boy was not named after his own father, family members expected him to be named after a grandfather or ancestor. As a token of affection, the name may have been that of a childless aunt or uncle. Finally, fashions in naming have exerted pressures of their own, whether directly or indirectly. Some parents may have chosen a name simply because it seemed popular at the time, while others have consciously tried to find a name that would express their own style and taste.

Of course, some of these limitations and traditions are still with us. For most of today's parents, however, the complexity of the naming process stems not from restrictions but from the range of possibilities open to them. Ideas for names can be drawn from all of the sources (and more) that we have cited—religious, national, ethnic, social, family, fashion, and others.

Under the circumstances, you along with other parents may feel that the task has grown too complicated. You suffer not from limited options but from too many of them. Maybe it's best to step back for a moment and consider naming from another viewpoint.

An old saying about parenthood goes like this: *There are two great gifts we give our children. One is roots. The other is wings.*

You may find it helpful to think about naming in the same way. A name is the first, the most personal, and possibly the most important gift that parents can offer. Unlike most other gifts, it is meant to last a lifetime.

Keeping this in mind is important because it means that the name has to wear well. It goes beyond the period of infancy, when the name is simply a sound to your new baby; beyond childhood, when the name may sometimes be a source of pride or of embarrassment; beyond adolescence and early adult life into maturity and old age. The name you give serves to establish an identity throughout a lifetime of major events and changes.

Choose the gift carefully—not only to commemorate the past but to celebrate the future.

The chapters that follow are intended to help you make your selection. Taken together, they don't comprise a book of rules to be rigidly followed—simply a guide based in large measure on the experience of other parents, today and in the past, who had to arrive at the same decision. In the end, though, the responsibility for judgment belongs to you. Here and there, we'll try to remind you that it's a joyful responsibility as well.

# 2. Factors to Keep in Mind When Choosing a Name

When parents choose a name for their baby, a principal consideration should be the harmony between the first name and the last name. Traditionally, the last name has meant the family name of the father, but in recent years there has been a growing trend among parents to give their children both maternal and paternal family names, with or without a hyphen, and occasionally to use the mother's family name as the last name. Actually, there's nothing new about including the mother's family name as a middle or even as a first name, and we'll discuss this possibility later. But its use as a last name is a relatively recent phenomenon, at least in this country.

Whichever family name is used, the parents should choose an appropriate first name to go with it. Although this point would probably win general agreement, it's not unusual to meet people whose names indicate that their parents either did not give full attention to the decision or else had some other goal in mind. This doesn't mean that something is wrong with the name they chose or with the family name, but that the *combination* of the two has failed to work out.

What's the explanation? To a large extent a preference in names is, like many other preferences, a matter of individual taste. In choosing a wardrobe, we pick the clothes that we find personally attractive. Nevertheless, it's also true that some styles, fabrics, or colors offer more harmonious combinations than others. When they don't work well together, attention is drawn to the separate identity of each. When a harmonious coming together does occur, the effect can make the whole appear greater than the sum of its parts.

The following principles may serve as navigational points in the selection process. Depending on your own orientation, you may attach varying degrees of importance to them, but a consideration of the entire group is one way to start.

## Listen to the Sound

How do the first and last names sound together? Is the sound smooth or choppy, pleasant or unsettling? One way to achieve an agreeable effect is through alliteration—using names that have the same initial sound. A famous example is *Marilyn Monroe*; the repetition also aids in recalling the name. However, the result may seem a bit contrived to some parents, especially if it's made even more emphatic, as with *James Joseph Jefferson*; others may feel that this effect is exactly what they're seeking. In either case, it's generally wise to keep the last letter as well as the initial letter of the first name in mind, so that the names don't disappear into each other. This possibility exists with names like *Alexandra Allen* or *Norman Nash*.

Other considerations of sound involve names that have similar endings. This may often be unintentional, and it's only apparent when the name is said aloud: *Janice Wallace*, *Brendan Nolan*, *Liza Kaiser*. A step further takes you into rhyming, and whether you like or dislike such names as *Jane Crane* or *Lawrence Torrence*, you may want to let them sit for a while before making a final decision. If you have a strong preference for a name even though it creates a rhyme, the use of a closely linked second name may offer a pleasant solution. For example, your daughter may eventually feel unhappy with *Mary Carey*, but she'll probably be comfortable with *Mary Louise Carey*, or *Marianne Carey*.

Remember, too, that names have hard and soft sounds, and one of each may be better than two of a kind. A family name like *Trask* or *Beck* may be softened with a first name like *Sarah* or *Arthur*.

## A Matter of Rhythm

Compare the number of syllables in each name. As a general rule, a longer last name is enhanced by a shorter first name and vice versa. To put it a different way, an unequal number of syllables in each name may be preferable to an equal number. Using a pair of earlier examples, another criticism of *Jane Crane* and *Lawrence Torrence* is that, in addition to rhyming, the names contain the same numbers of syllables, giving a repetitious effect. They take on new luster when switched around: *Jane Torrence*, *Lawrence Crane*.

Here, as elsewhere, the objection may be raised that there are many famous exceptions, as indeed there are. Novelist *Pearl Buck*, movie star *Humphrey Bogart*, and fashion designer *Gloria Vanderbilt* are just three of the large number of well-known people whose first and last names have the same number of syllables. Whether they would have preferred a different arrangement is anyone's guess.

## Pronouncing the Name

One of the most uncomfortable situations for children beginning school is when their teacher and classmates have difficulty getting their name right. Obviously, not everything can be or should be made simple, but it shouldn't be needlessly complicated either. Constant mispronunciation may lead a person to drop the first name and adopt the middle name instead (a move that may be made for other reasons as well). The problem is particularly noticeable when both first and last names are difficult to say, but it may also apply in the case of apparently simple first names. For example, the Scottish name for *John* consists of only three letters, *Ian*, but this name, increasingly popular in the United States, may be heard as *Eye-on*, *Ee-an*, or *Yan*, among other pronunciations (the second is correct).

This is not meant to suggest that *Ian* or other attractive and unusual first names should not be given consideration by parents, but perhaps when the family name itself is difficult to pronounce, a more familiar first name should be given.

## Check the Spelling

As with pronunciation, a key question to ask is whether a difficult-to-spell name will hinder your child on the journey through life. Even if you've had similar experiences with your own name, a clear response may not come immediately. With the passage of time, we tend to grow accustomed to minor obstacles; anticipating them may even become a reflex action. In the countless daily situations where you have to give your name, do you say automatically, "I'll spell that for you"?

This is generally more true of family names than of first names, but if the possibility already exists, you needn't compound the problem. On the other hand, ease of pronunciation and spelling are not the only criteria for naming. If this were true, we'd all have simple, one-syllable first names.


## Nothing Too Fancy—or Funny

Another potential risk is a name that seems fanciful or pretentious. While names from mythology like *Diomedes* and *Eurydice*, or weighty medieval names like *Athelstan* and *Guinevere*, may work out for some children, they are certain to be a cause of comment. More often than not, such names are also difficult to say and spell.

At the same time, parents needn't ignore the opportunity to formulate a slightly unusual name. One way to do this is to use a variation of a familiar name; some names have many more than others. For example, *Amy* doesn't offer much room for experiment, but an equally short and simple name like *Carol* has a long list of variations: *Carla*, *Carly*, *Carola*, *Carolyn*, *Caryl*, to name just a few. The chapters on girls' and boys' names contain listings of variations for most major names.

A different name can also be created by combining aspects of each parent's first name, so long as a graceful result is achieved. A girl born to *Teresa* and *Joseph*, for example, can be named *Terry Jo*. (Incidentally, most such name combinations seem to be given to girls rather than to boys.) Again, parents may want to consider setting off a short and common family name with a more formal first name, adding the benefit of unequal syllables mentioned earlier. In this way, *Alice Brown* can be transformed to *Alexandra Brown*, *Ralph Smith* can become *Bradford Smith*.

With incongruous or pretentious names, the danger is that they may slide toward the comical. We've already seen this risk with rhyming names. Some parents may believe that these and other more deliberately "joking" names are genuinely funny. Everyone is probably familiar with names in this category; among the many examples of real, or supposedly real, combinations are *Rose Busch*, *Hedda Hare*, *Kelly Green*, *Jack Potts*, *Woody Grove*, *Candy Kane*, *Heather Fields*, and many more.

Perhaps the only thing to say about these names is that nothing grows stale more quickly than a joke repeated over and over. As with other aspects of naming, the best advice is to let your own common sense be your guide.

## This Year's Fashions

A reference to fashion implies that something is currently popular. This aspect of naming is illustrated in chapter 3, which features lists of the top ten names. Some parents may not be concerned about—or even aware of—the popularity of the name they have selected. Those who are concerned either favor fashionable names or prefer to avoid them.

It's important to emphasize that saying a name is in or out of fashion carries no reflection on the name itself. This year's *Jennifer*, *Jessica*, and *Melissa* are neither more nor less attractive than the *Dorothy*, *Helen*, and *Margaret* of yesteryear. When we note that a name has recently gained or lost favor, the intention is not to pass judgment on the name but to provide information to parents. If you find a name appealing in all other respects, its standing in the popularity polls may not weigh heavily in your decision.

Two related points about fashions in naming are worthy of mention. As we'll see later, many names are not just individually popular but are part of a more general trend. One recent trend is a return to biblical names: for girls, names like *Sarah*, *Rebecca*, and *Rachel*; for boys, *Michael*, *David*, and *Daniel*. Similar trends—involving names of Greek and Roman, English, French, or Spanish origin—can be traced in earlier periods. An awareness of these trends may be helpful in making a selection.

In addition, it's interesting to note that the popularity of some names, whatever their derivation, seems to survive all changes in style and fashion. In this category are names like *Elizabeth*, *Mary*, and *Katharine*; *James*, *Robert*, and *John*, along with their many variations. These are the perennials.

## Unisex Names: For or Against?

The pool of available names includes many that have been and still may be used for both girls and boys. In general, four groups are involved.

The first consists of names whose masculine and feminine variations have been drawn essentially from the same source. For example, *Antonia* and *Anthony* are both derived from the Roman clan name *Antonius*. In other instances, the feminine and masculine versions of names have evolved more or less at the same time; two currently popular examples are *Christina/Christian* and *Nicole/Nicholas*. A second category consists of names that were once masculine and are now mostly feminine (*Ashley*,

*Robin*, *Shelley*). There are also names that were once used more or less equally for both sexes, especially in England, but are now almost entirely feminine (*Beverly*, *Marion*, *Evelyn*). Finally, there are the genuinely unisex names, such as *Stacy*, *Leslie*, *Terry*, and others.

One argument sometimes heard in favor of unisex names is that they allow parents to reach a definite naming decision before knowing the sex of their child. This seems to be a reversal of priorities. The important thing is that the name is appropriate—and not how early it is given.

## Religious Traditions

As we noted earlier, the influence of religion on naming practices is very old. Religious requirements affect naming less today than in the past, and in some faiths custom has changed greatly over the last century. It's wise to ask at your local church or temple about any guidelines you may be expected to follow in naming your child.

## Give a Thought to Nicknames

The term originally meant "an additional name," without any reflection on the merit of the name. Obviously, you can't foresee what nickname your child may end up having, because so many possibilities are involved. Some nicknames may be derived from given names, so that *Kathy* and *Tom* are likely choices for children named *Katharine* or *Thomas*. But nicknames may also be based on family names, an incident in childhood, an episode in school, physical characteristics, and many other things difficult to foresee.

One thing parents can do, however, is to realize in

advance that some names may be twisted by a child's playmates. For instance, the respectable old name *Cecil*, originally a Roman clan name and one borne by such luminaries as Hollywood director Cecil B. De Mille, may be turned into *Sissy*; the charming *Wendy* may become *Windy*; and a lovely *Miranda* will wish she had never heard of Snow White after the endless repetition of "*Mira, Mira*, on the wall. . . ." Fortunately, many of these nicknames don't last beyond early school days.

## P.S.—Don't Skip the Initials

In addition to saying the name and spelling it out, it's a good idea to write it as a monogram, the way it might appear on stationery, luggage, or jewelry. This only takes a minute, and it allows you to be sure that potentially embarrassing combinations of initials—B.A.T., S.A.P., F.A.T., H.A.M., to give but a few—do not trail your child throughout life.

# 3. The Top Ten

You may or may not feel strongly about the popularity of the names you tentatively select for your baby before making a final choice. However, if the choice is a difficult one, whether or not a name is in or out of fashion may be a deciding factor. Most people are interested in naming trends and in knowing which names are at the top of the popularity polls. Not so long ago, gathering and analyzing such information was a major undertaking, but it has been speeded up considerably in today's computer age.

In this country, there are three principal sources of information for the lists of so-called top ten names. The first consists of reports prepared and published by government agencies, ranging from the Social Security Administration to state and local health departments. In New York City, for example, the health department has issued such reports periodically since the turn of the century, based on birth certificate registrations. But public agencies are interested more in numbers and totals than in the names themselves. Thus, a second and related source of information is comprised of studies of the same collections of data by research teams or individuals, who have a particular interest in the subject. As an example, researchers have compared names registered in the same groups of counties at different time intervals in order to follow trends. Finally, public opinion polls and consumer surveys of parents have been conducted in an effort to determine name popularity.

For the time periods indicated, here is a compilation of the results obtained:

## Top Ten Names for Girls

| *1900* | *1925* | *1950* | *Early 1980s* |
|---|---|---|---|
| Mary | Mary | Linda | Jennifer |
| Margaret | Dorothy | Mary | Jessica |
| Catherine | Margaret | Patricia | Melissa |
| Elizabeth | Anne | Susan | Sarah |
| Anne | Helen | Deborah | Nicole |
| Dorothy | Elizabeth | Kathleen | Michelle |
| Ruth | Catherine | Barbara | Elizabeth |
| Helen | Ruth | Nancy | Christina |
| Rose | Barbara | Carol | Stephanie |
| Frances | Jean | Sharon | Katherine |

Of all girls' names in the top ten, only two, *Elizabeth* and *Catherine/Katherine* appear on the lists for both the first and the most recent time periods shown. Only the latter is on all four lists, and possibly it maintained its hold through its ability to change form to *Kathleen* and then to *Katherine* (which is really an older form of the name). It may also be argued that since *Nancy* is a variation of *Anne*, this name should at least be credited with making three out of four lists. The suggestion illustrates one of the difficulties of following trends in naming: how to decide when a name variation has established its independence to the extent that it merits separate consideration. For our purposes, let's not take up that problem but instead accept *Anne* and *Nancy* as different names.

A closer analysis reveals that the change in naming seems to accelerate over time. The period from 1900 to 1925, while it shows modifications in ranking, indicates little overall change in substance: eight names are carried over from one list to another, and *Rose* and *Frances* are replaced by *Barbara* and *Jean*. A more rapid pace is found in the period from 1925 to 1950. Only three names are carried over: *Mary*, *Barbara*, and *Catherine/Kathleen*. Finally, in the period from 1950 to the early 1980s, only *Kathleen/Katherine* appears on both lists; otherwise the change is complete.

Turning to the boys' lists, we see that there are some similarities to the changes in the lists of girls' names, but also some important differences.

## Top Ten Names for Boys

| *1900* | *1925* | *1950* | *Early 1980s* |
|---|---|---|---|
| John | John | Robert | Michael |
| William | Robert | James | Christopher |
| Charles | William | Michael | Jason |
| Joseph | James | John | David |
| Robert | Charles | David | Brian |
| Edward | Joseph | William | James |
| James | Richard | Joseph | Robert |
| George | George | Thomas | Matthew |
| Samuel | Thomas | Richard | Joseph |
| Thomas | Edward | Stephen | John |

While only one girl's name (*Catherine* and its variations) stayed in the top-ten listing over the entire period,
four names for boys—*John, Joseph, Robert,* and *James*—
appear on all four lists. The period from 1900 to 1925,
as with the girls' names, shows little change, with a carry-
over of nine names and only one substitution—*Richard*
for *Samuel.* For 1925 to 1950, there is a replacement of
four names and a carry-over of six: *John, Robert, William, James, Joseph,* and *Richard.* For the last two periods compared, six names—*Robert, James, Michael,
John, David,* and *Joseph*—again appear on both lists.

In other words, the changes in naming patterns for
boys are less evident than for girls and also occur at a
slower pace.

Incidentally, the fact that a name no longer appears in
the top-ten listing does not necessarily mean that it has
dropped dramatically in popularity. Often different forms
of names like *Elizabeth* (*Liza* or *Lisa*) and *Mary* (*Marie,
Maura*) hover at the border of the top ten without quite
making it into the inner circle. This is less true of boys'
than of girls' names, where a greater variation is found.
Also, many "new" names—new for a given time period—sometimes remain just beyond the top ten for several years before advancing or falling behind. Today this
category includes girls' names like *Tiffany, Danielle,
Heather, Amanda, Erin,* and *Amy*; and for boys, *Anthony,
Eric, Jeffrey, Ryan, Sean,* and *Justin.*

It should also be noted that the changes in individual
names may not apply to the types of names that are
popular at any particular time. Although some biblical
names are dropped from the list, others are added; the
same observation applies to names that have a Greek
origin. Using the preceding lists for comparison, the principal declines have occurred in names of Latin, Old German, and Old English origins. As an interesting sidelight,

the Hebrew *Deborah* (1950), which means "bee," has been replaced in the early 1980s by the Greek *Melissa*, which has the same meaning. This is no doubt a coincidence, but it illustrates the fact that a surface change does not necessarily mean a change in substance.

A second type of comparison is to match these national samples with a smaller sample of names, based on births to a group of parents in the early 1980s. My sample consists of a total of 412, including 212 names for girls and 200 names for boys.

## Top Ten Names for Girls: Early 1980s

| *Study Sample* | *National Sample* |
|---|---|
| Christina | Jennifer |
| Katherine | Jessica |
| Laura | Melissa |
| Elizabeth | Sarah |
| Sarah | Nicole |
| Rebecca | Michelle |
| Anne | Elizabeth |
| Rachel | Christina |
| Michelle | Stephanie |
| Megan | Katherine |

There are five correspondences between the study sample and the national sample—*Christina*, *Katherine*, *Elizabeth*, *Sarah*, and *Michelle*. Other names that were also nationally popular but outside the top ten enjoyed a greater degree of popularity with these parents (for example, *Laura* and *Rebecca*). Note also that the most popular name nationally, *Jennifer*, does not appear at all in the top-ten study sample.

## Top Ten Names for Boys: Early 1980s

| *Study Sample* | *National Sample* |
| --- | --- |
| Michael | Michael |
| John | Christopher |
| David | Jason |
| Daniel | David |
| Matthew | Brian |
| Jesse | James |
| Paul | Robert |
| Ryan | Matthew |
| Brendan | Joseph |
| Joseph | John |

As with the rankings for girls, five of the same names appear on both listings—*Michael*, *John*, *David*, *Matthew*, and *Joseph*. Here, the top-ranking name, *Michael*, is the same on both.

Overall, 64 of the 212 girls' names (or 30 percent) in the study sample corresponded with names in the national sample, while 80 of 200 boys' names (40 percent) corresponded. To put it another way, boys' names in the study sample were more likely to be found in the national top-ten listing than were names for girls in the study sample.

What do these results tell us about naming patterns since 1900? First, they demonstrate that the pace of change in naming has accelerated considerably over the past century, just as it has in most other aspects of society. From one generation to the next, naming patterns are likely to shift much more rapidly than they did in the past. Part of the explanation is simply the greater mobility—be it geographic, economic, or social—that exists today. But more than anything else, many researchers suggest that the growth of the mass media has had the largest single impact on naming. Since the 1920s the advent of radio, recordings, movies, television, and videotape not only has added enormously to the available pool of names but has brought them almost instant attention nationally and internationally. This attention, in turn, has itself influenced the names we choose.

At the same time the comparisons indicate a second conclusion. These changes in naming patterns occur more frequently for girls than for boys. In addition, parents appear to use more individual variation in naming daughters than they do in naming sons. This more conservative attitude toward boys' names has persisted despite the overall impact of the mass media.

# 4. Reasons for the Choice

When we looked at guidelines for name selection, the principal focus was on avoiding pitfalls—recognizing in advance that some names and combinations may be less appropriate than others. Now we'll take a different approach, reviewing the possible *influences* on the naming decision. As with the guidelines, the degree to which you are affected by these various elements will depend on your own background and attitudes. If family tradition is an important consideration for you, the influence of other factors will be greatly reduced. However, if there are no compelling reasons to make a particular choice, some of the following categories may be helpful as resources in drawing up your preliminary list of names.

## Staying Within the Family

Naming patterns based on family custom go back very far in history. The practice of passing on first names from grandfather to grandson was followed by some families in ancient Greece and predated the naming of son for father. In aristocratic Roman families, the names of boys always included both the *gens* or clan name and the family name, as in *Julius* (clan) *Caesar* (family); his first name was *Gaius*. The clan name was also used as a first name for girls. Both Caesar's sister and daughter were named *Julia*, and other feminine first names that were originally clan names include *Cecilia*, *Lucy*, and *Marcia*.

In addition, many names within a family may be a matter of choice rather than long tradition. Taking a child's middle or first name from the mother's family name, or an adaptation of it, became fashionable in nineteenth-century America and may be having a small revival today (more on this in the next chapter). A child's name may recall that of a famous ancestor, as when *Louis Napoleon Bonaparte*'s name evoked the memory of his celebrated uncle, or when the future United States statesman *Benjamin Harrison* was named for his great-grandfather, a signer of the Declaration of Independence. This kind of naming not only honors the ancestor but calls attention to the child's heritage, sometimes with great success. Louis Napoleon eventually became president and then emperor of France, and Benjamin Harrison was elected the twenty-third United States president.

An ancestor or relative need not have achieved fame in order to be commemorated in this way. Most families have a particularly admired or beloved grandparent, aunt, or uncle who would be greatly pleased to learn that a new baby will bear his or her name. The problem facing parents whose choice falls in this direction is that, with decreasing family size, the number of relatives may exceed the supply of new babies ready for naming. Inevitably, some relatives will be disappointed, even though they keep their feelings concealed. Parents should also be certain that the name itself meets their own desires, apart from its family associations.

Another way of keeping names within the family was touched on earlier: both parents' first names can be used in combination, some of them less obvious than others. A girl born to *Patricia* and *Lawrence*, may be named *Patricia Lauren*, *Laura Patrice*, or *Tricia Loren*, to give just a few possibilities. Choices for boys include *Lawrence Patrick*, *Patrick Lawrence*, *Lorne Patrick*, and *Patric Lorn*, among others.

The most familiar parent-to-child naming practice, of course, involves bestowing the parent's name exactly as it is. This affects boys more than girls and brings up the various aspects of the "Junior question." A boy's name need not be identical in order to bring up this question. To take one of the illustrations cited above, a boy named *Lawrence Patrick* would not be a *Jr.* if his father's name was *Lawrence Paul*. Although the danger still exists that they might be called *Little Larry* and *Big Larry* (and later *Young Larry* and *Old Larry*), a different distinction is usually attempted early on. For example, the son may be referred to as *Pat*, while the father retains *Lawrence*.

If the names are identical, however, parents must be prepared not only for the *Little/Big*, *Young/Old* possibilities but also for the customary *Larry Jr.* and even *Junie*. As we've stressed more than once, this is a question for parents to decide based on personal preference—including some consideration of the possible future preferences of the child.

According to most researchers, the use of *Jr.* is declining among today's parents, although no specific reasons are cited. Probably, as with other fashions in naming, the decline is simply a result of overuse. It should be added that since few systematic studies have been done, comparative figures are seldom available. In my own study sample of 200 boys' names, there were 15 examples of *Jr.*, or 7.5 percent. A larger study done in the 1950s reported a rate of 18 percent, meaning that the proportion in the current sample is less than half of that noted thirty years ago. Moreover, only 5 of the 212 girls in the sample (approximately 2.3 percent) had the same first names as their mothers.

## The Place of Siblings

A separate aspect of family influences remains to be considered. If the new baby already has an older sister or brother, or if a younger one is anticipated in the future, should the names of the children complement each other? (This may be a more urgent decision in the case of a multiple pregnancy, but only about one of every ninety expectant couples has to contemplate this eventuality.) Some parents deal with the question by ignoring it as long as the name selected for each child is the product of a thoughtful discussion. Others view the naming decision as part of a larger pattern.

It may turn out to be a boy-girl pattern as with *John* and *Joanna*, *Mark* and *Marcia*. If even larger numbers are a possibility, parents may wish to have available a group of names beginning with the same sound (*Elizabeth*, *Elias*, *Elaine*, *Elliott*, *Eleanor*) or simply the same letter (*Madeline*, *Matthew*, *Melanie*, *Michael*). Among same-sex groups (the tendency is greater when naming girls), clusters of similar names may seem attractive, as with the Puritan favorites *Faith*, *Hope*, and *Charity* or the more modern *Lily*, *Daisy*, and *Rose*. Whatever you may think of name clusters, at least they represent a step beyond the Roman custom of naming by number, especially above four: *Quintus/Quinta*, *Sextus/Sexta*, *Septimus/Septima*, and *Octavius/Octavia* were names for boys and girls.

Siblings may also play a more active role in name selection. In my study sample a number of couples said that older children had been involved in choosing a name for the baby, either by reviewing groups of names or by making their own suggestions. When this happened, the name finally chosen was one of those given the stamp of approval by the older child.

## Events of Pregnancy and Birth

General or specific factors associated with childbirth may influence the naming process. These may range from circumstances at the assumed moment of conception (date, place, setting) through pregnancy to the moment of the child's entry into the world. This last factor is rare nowadays, when nearly all parents have already made their choice, but in earlier times it often affected naming. As described in the Old Testament, for example, *Isaac* ("laughing one") was named because of his appearance at birth, and *Jacob* ("following after") came quickly after his twin brother, *Esau*.

The city of birth may be used for a name, as indicated by the reference to *Florence* Nightingale in the listing of names for girls. Some months (*April*, *May*, *June*) have served as girls' names since early in the present century. A few names mark particular holidays, as *Natalie* and *Noel* indicate Christmas. The names *Dominic* or *Dominique* may single out a boy or girl born on Sunday, although they may be used generally as well. Other possibilities can be found in the chapters of names for girls and boys.

In more personal terms, some couples may wish to name their baby after a person who has played an important role around the time of birth. This may involve a middle name (as discussed in chapter 5) or even the first name. A number of parents with whom I spoke told me that they had changed their naming plan because of the special degree of help provided by a physician, nurse, midwife, or friend.

## A Desire for Roots

The success of Alex Haley's book *Roots* and the television series created from it symbolized a desire on the part not only of black Americans but of those from many other ethnic groups to rediscover and celebrate their heritage. Part of this heritage includes names neglected until recently: for those of African descent, boys' names like *Oto*, *Kwame*, *Jomo*; girls names like *Akuba*, *Keisha*, *Tamike*. Jewish parents have added names from Israel to the existing pool of biblical names: *Chaim*, *Yaron*, *Ariel* for boys; *Dalia*, *Yael*, *Tamar* for girls. Still other names— European, Hispanic, Asian—have expanded the choices of parents in these various groups.

Most of these names will probably never enter the mainstream of United States naming patterns. By definition, the most popular names are those that appeal to the broadest cross-section of American parents. At the same time, names that clearly derive from a particular ethnic or religious group have been transmitted from one culture to another for many centuries, not just in America but throughout the world. You can trace this international movement of names in the chapter on historical trends.

For now, it may be interesting to note that names from three different cultures have had a major influence on naming practices in the United States over the past several years. Perhaps the leading group consists of Hebrew and Aramaic names from the Bible: *Rebecca*, *Rachel*, *Sarah*,

*Abigail; Daniel, Joshua, David, Jacob*, to cite just a few. A second group is comprised of Celtic names, primarily Irish and Scottish: *Colleen, Megan, Tara, Maura; Sean, Colin, Kevin, Brendan*. Finally, a third and much smaller group is made up of French variations or names that are Old French in origin: *Michelle, Stephanie, Nicole; Andre, Byron*.

It may be inaccurate to suggest that in selecting a name from these or other ethnic groups not their own, parents are demonstrating a desire for roots. But in a range of different ways and using a variety of expressions—"traditional," "solid," "old-fashioned"—parents in the study sample often seemed to indicate that this was the case.

## Favorites From History

Naming a child after a famous historical personage is another very old cultural pattern. Many Romans took *Gaius* or *Julius* (or *Julian*) from Caesar's name; Christians throughout the Mediterranean world adopted the name of the Emperor *Constantine* after he officially accepted the practice of Christianity; the names of *Charles* the Great (Charlemagne) and *William* the Conqueror were borrowed for countless namesakes in the Middle Ages. In similar fashion, American parents honored their own heroes: often both names were taken from presidents, like *George Washington, Thomas Jefferson, Andrew Jackson*, and others. In recent years, perhaps the only United States president who has had the same influence on naming is *John Fitzgerald Kennedy*.

The influences mentioned here mainly affected boys' names, but girls were named for the same personages as well: *Julia* for Julius Caesar, *Constantia* for Constantine, *Carol* or *Charlotte* for *Charles*. Women also had their own heroines: the medieval Queen *Margaret* of Scotland;

the French *Joan* of Arc; queens *Mary* and *Elizabeth* of England, two empresses of Russia named *Catherine*.

In our own day, this aspect of naming seems less prevalent here and in other Western countries. Among the births in the study sample, no child was named for a generally recognizable historical figure. Possibly the only exceptions involved a small group of Eastern European and Hispanic parents who had given their sons the names of past heroes within those cultures. These were classified as "root" names rather than as "historical" names, based on the definition that a historical name had to be familiar outside its own culture.

On the other hand, a potentially large group of names may be borrowed from well-known people in a different area: celebrities and personalities from movies, television, theater, sports, etc. The key difference here is that a name from history calls attention to itself: parents want others to know that a child is named for this particular person. With celebrity names, I've found that parents seldom indicate that any direct link is involved. The most frequent comment from parents was that they "liked the name," not that they were naming their child after a particular celebrity.

## Favorite Characters

As with historical names, the use of mythological or fictional characters for naming children has long been an option for parents. Beginning in our own childhood, most of us have acquired a group of favorites whose names can be set aside for that purpose. The problem is usually that when the child arrives both parents have an abundance of names; in the end, they may settle on one that doesn't appear on either list.

My own experience is that the current availability of

an enormous name bank—more names than were ever offered to parents at any time in the past—makes it difficult to show a cause-and-effect relationship. As an example, let's look at the current popularity of the girl's name *Ashley*. It was originally an English place name meaning "ash tree meadow." As with many similar names, it became a family name and then a first name for boys. Probably its most familiar use in fiction occurred when the novelist Margaret Mitchell selected it for one of the leading male characters in *Gone With the Wind*. The film version, released in 1939 and still shown periodically on television, brought it to the attention of millions.

Since *Gone With the Wind* is supposed to have had an influence on naming patterns in the 1940s, it would seem logical to assume that the subsequent TV releases played some role in keeping the name before the public. But while the *Ashley* character was masculine, all of the parents with whom I discussed it assumed that *Ashley* was a feminine name. This was true not only of the three couples who selected the name for their daughters but of a number of others with whom I spoke.

It suggests that contrary to the opinion of some researchers, the names of the original fictional characters may not always affect naming practices directly. Instead, they may enter the consciousness of parents in a gradual process—for example, by means of a subsequent TV dramatic series in which the name of a character or of a performer has been borrowed or adapted from the earlier work.

## Other Resources

Many other possibilities are available to parents for name selection, and we've tried to cover them in the chapters on girls' and boys' names. Some parents may be influenced by the attributes or basic meanings of names. These may be apparent at first glance: *Brooke*, *Dawn*, *Melody*; *Victor*, *Robin*, *Scott*. Or a little more investigation may be necessary to learn the meaning of other names: *Andrew* ("manly"), *Eric* ("ruler"), *Kenneth* ("handsome"), *Neil* ("champion"); *Amanda* ("lovable"), *Iris* ("rainbow"), *Nadine* ("hope"), *Shana* ("beautiful").

You may be interested in names from nature—flowers and plants, trees, birds and animals, jewel names, colors. Geographical names may be an option—cities, states, rivers, other place names. Whatever the area of choice, you should begin your list as soon as possible—no matter how the decision will turn out eventually. Many examples are offered in chapters 8 and 9, as well as in the index.

# 5. What About the Middle Name?

In America, giving a middle name to a child is a fairly recent naming practice. It began about two hundred years ago and became widely accepted only in the present century. A simple way of illustrating the growth of this trend is to use the succession of United States presidents. We have had forty presidents, but there are only thirty-nine names, because Grover Cleveland appears twice (his terms were not consecutive). Incidentally, *Grover* was his middle name; he dropped the use of his first name, *Stephen*.

Neither of the two presidents in the eighteenth century, George Washington and John Adams, had a middle name. In the nineteenth century, ranging from Thomas Jefferson to William McKinley, eight of twenty-two presidents—fewer than half—had middle names. But from Theodore Roosevelt to Ronald Reagan in our own century, thirteen of fifteen presidents have had middle names, and one of the two others at least had a middle initial, even if there was no name attached to it. As the story goes, Harry *S* Truman received the initial when there was a family disagreement about which grandparent's name should be used; both of them began with *S*, which represented a compromise.

Moreover, of the presidents since Mr. Truman left the White House, *all* have had middle names: Dwight *David* Eisenhower, John *Fitzgerald* Kennedy, Lyndon *Baines* Johnson, Richard *Milhous* Nixon, Gerald *Rudolph* Ford, James *Earl* Carter, Ronald *Wilson* Reagan.

A look at the origins of presidential middle names shows that five had their father's first name as a middle name; six received a regular second name along with the first (although some of these may have been given for family reasons); and nine had their mother's family name. The very first of the middle-name presidents, John *Quincy* Adams, was given the name of a maternal great-grandfather; his mother's name was Smith.

When parents are considering a middle name, do any special factors arise? Although most of the reasons for bestowing first names apply equally to middle names, a few additional points can be made. Perhaps the major difference between middle and first names is that the decision is less critical; indeed, parents can avoid picking a middle name entirely if they wish. However, it's also true that as middle names have become more solidly established, we've grown to expect them. A child without a middle name today is probably just as unusual as a child who was the sole possessor of one in earlier times.

Still, some parents veto a middle name. They may feel that since it is seldom used, except when filling out forms and applications, it is little more than excess baggage. Others may view the emphasis on a middle name as pretentious, an argument that was raised two centuries ago in America, when middle names were just being introduced.

On the other hand, parents who have a positive view of middle names see them as a way of enriching the naming process. For one thing, the middle name offers a second choice, not only for the parents but for the child, who for one reason or another may later decide to use the middle name rather than the first.

Aside from this consideration, there may be family or personal reasons for adding a middle name. If the desire to honor a family member with a first name may cause hurt feelings on the part of another relative, the middle name offers a way out. It can be useful when parents are strongly urged to consider a name traditional in the family but feel just as strongly that they want to make their own choice. And parents may also find the middle name unexpectedly handy for showing their thanks to a relative or friend who, late in pregnancy or around the time of birth, offers extra support and assistance at a critical moment.

Even if no pressing reasons are involved, the middle name can expand the basic selection of a first name when there is a link between the two. With historical names, for example, it's possible for parents to use not only one but both elements, as with *Martin Luther* King, *John Calvin* Coolidge (President Coolidge kept *John* for a rainy day), scientist *George Washington* Carver, and former Pacific Fleet Admiral *Ulysses Simpson Grant* Sharp, named for the eighteenth president. Some names also seem to accompany each other naturally: *Anne Marie*, *John Joseph*, *Mary Beth*, *James Edward*. Often in such cases, both names are regularly used for and by the child, although this happens more frequently with girls than with boys.

A different effect can be created by varying first and middle name combinations. For boys, this meant until recently that a familiar name would be used first and a less familiar name second, whereas the opposite was true for girls. Now it seems that both boys' and girls' names are treated in the same way, with the middle name serving as a backup to the first: *Courtney Anne*, *Jeremy Paul*, *Shannon Lee*, *Scott Michael*.

Remember that at some point either name may turn into an initial. In the past the word "initial" was seldom seen without its chaperon "middle," but the trend toward use of a first initial is still with us, and some women as well as men are following it. *Miranda Jean* may become either *Miranda J.* or *M. Jean*.

Naturally, you needn't limit your selection to only one middle name if you have reasons for adding another. This practice has never been common among American parents, but there are certainly regional examples of it. Admiral *Ulysses S. Grant* Sharp, mentioned above, no doubt has southern counterparts named for the other Civil War commanding general, *Robert E. Lee*. However, most such additional names are seldom used.

In my study sample, middle names were given by a large majority of parents—approximately 85 percent. The actual proportion is probably even higher, since a number of parents who failed to write the names may well have given them. As with first names, the sources of middle names are extremely varied, so the analysis was limited to only two factors: use of the father's first name as a middle name for boys or the mother's first name as a middle name for girls, and use of the mother's family name as a middle name for either a son or a daughter.

The results showed that some 15 percent of parents who gave a middle name used the family name of the mother, while a slightly smaller percentage—11 percent—used a parental first name. The mother's family name was given slightly more often to girls than to boys, and the father's first name was given about twice as often to boys as the mother's first name was given to girls. Possibly this demonstrates that the *Jr.* effect, even when it's secondary, is still greater among boys.

# 6. Do Our Names Influence Our Lives?

Names evoke images and impressions in our minds. Some may be positive, some negative, and some may be vague and uncertain—blanks waiting to be filled in by experience. Favorable impressions are typically associated with popular names, although, as with the chicken and the egg, it's sometimes difficult to know which came first. Positive feelings may also extend beyond individual names to name categories. In recent years, as we've noted, biblical names have returned to favor, whether as a result of the desire for roots, religious factors, the magnetism of fashion, or for other reasons.

But this observation fails to explain why some biblical names are preferred over others. Parents who quickly choose *Rachel* or *Joshua*, for example, are unlikely to consider *Bashemath* or *Hezekiah*. The obvious objection is that such names are more difficult to say and to spell. Naturally, these are important considerations—and yet if, for any reason, the names suddenly became fashionable, we'd soon learn how to spell them. *Algernon* and *Ernestine* are no more difficult to spell than *Christopher* and *Stephanie*, but they are seldom encountered today,

36

while the latter two names are great favorites.

Given a list of simple first names, most of us could respond to them without much prodding. What lies behind these favorable or unfavorable reactions?

## Familiar vs. Unfamiliar

A major reason for having a negative attitude toward a particular name is that it represents an unknown quantity. We tend to be more comfortable with names that are familiar to us. This is demonstrated by the enduring preference for names like *Anne* and *John* and the recurring popularity of *Sarah* and *David*. However, the name shouldn't become overly familiar in a brief period of time; those that enjoy a rapid rise in popularity generally have a rapid fall as well (*Lana* and *Vicki*, *Travis* and *Dylan*).

If we encounter a new name, we usually judge it by the sound and the visual arrangement of letters—just as children do. In other words, our response takes place on a very basic level. Evidently, it has little to do with the name's actual meaning; in most cases we're unaware of what that meaning is.

In studies of attitudes toward names, mostly among grade school children, *Phoebe* and *Percival* were in a group of names labeled "weak and passive," according to the researchers. *Phoebe*, from Greek mythology, means "shining one" and is another of the many names, like *Cynthia* and *Delia*, given to the goddess of the moon and the hunt, known to the Romans as *Diana*. *Percival*, originally a French name meaning "pierce the valley," was a valiant knight in medieval tales centering around the quest for the Holy Grail; he is also the hero of Richard Wagner's opera *Parsifal*.

How could these two names be described as "weak

and passive"? It can happen only if we know nothing about them. But even when we do have additional information, does it change that initial impression? Perhaps some parents looking for older, more classical names would be willing to give *Phoebe* or *Percival* further consideration, while others would prefer to look elsewhere. As one character remarked of another's trumpet-playing in an old comedy sketch, "Even if that was good I wouldn't like it!"

The importance of familiarity is also illustrated by two other names that researchers found to be undesirable, *Benjamin* and *Nicole*. In view of their recent popularity, how can this classification be explained? The mystery is solved when we learn that the study in question was conducted in the 1960s, before the names began their rise in fashion. At that time they were unfamiliar to the children in the study, who reacted accordingly.

## Positive and Negative Associations

In discussing the reasons for choosing a name, we reviewed some of the positive associations that may be involved in the selection: famous names from the past, from literature, from the world of current stars and celebrities. There are also negative associations involved with names from these sources; they offer villains as well as heroes.

An unmistakable example is *Judas* (but not *Jude*), the disciple who betrayed Jesus and made his own name synonymous with "traitor." (A second-century B.C. hero of Israel was *Judas Maccabeus*, who is always identified by both names.) In American history, a similar notoriety was acquired during the Revolutionary War by *Benedict Arnold*, who attempted to surrender the fort of West Point to the British. The murderous Queen *Jezebel* received a terrible punishment for her idolatry and other crimes described in the Old Testament. From this same source novelist Charles Dickens borrowed the names of some of his most memorable villains: for example, *Uriah* Heep in *David Copperfield* and, until his belated change in character, *Ebenezer* Scrooge in *A Christmas Carol*.

Parents seldom consider these names. But there is another and much larger group of names whose associations are not exactly negative but possibly a bit too specific. They include names that have received wide attention through the media in the form of advertising (*Elsie* the Cow), comic strips and cartoons (*Donald* Duck, *Felix* the Cat, *Ferdinand* the Bull), popular songs (*Rudolph* the Red-Nosed Reindeer), and other sources. Generally, they are removed from the list of potential choices only as long as the particular association is fresh in the mind of the public. In the early 1900s, for example, the huge success of a comic strip character named Barney Google, also a popular song, made *Barney* an unlikely first-name choice of parents. Recently, however, its use for sympathetic characters in TV dramas seems to have helped considerably in its rehabilitation.

The same phenomenon can occur with names that appear to be firmly entrenched in slang usage. For more than two centuries, the name *Moll* or *Molly*, an Irish form of *Mary*, was synonymous with a criminal or a companion of criminals, as in "gun moll." Now the slang term is old-fashioned, and *Molly* is among the group of Irish names given special preference by parents. At several times in the past and for somewhat similar reasons, the same fate has seemed about to overtake the name *Jack*, but it has usually been successful in resisting a negative image.

## From Our Personal Experience

Some attitudes toward names are shared by many people, as with most of the examples mentioned above, but some are highly individual. These may be linked to personal experience, generally in childhood or the teen years. Again, these associations may be positive or negative: an early playmate, a next-door neighbor, a first love; a strict teacher, a school bully, someone to whom we lost a key sports event or school competition.

If the name is a common one and we meet others whose names are similar, its special quality may gradually fade over time, although the memory remains. On the other hand, whether a name is common or unique, it may become closely attached to *that* person. No subsequent encounters with others can alter the impressions it has created.

## Attitudes and Influences

Granted that most of us have these prejudices, how strongly can they influence our attitudes toward people who bear the names?

One measure of the importance of names is shown by the attention that advertising agencies, television networks, and producers of TV series pay to name selection. Whether the name is associated with a product or with characters in a dramatic series, possible names are often previewed with sample audiences in an effort to gauge public reaction. Authors give careful thought to the choice of their characters' names, hoping that the result will serve to establish their creations solidly in the reader's mind. Performers change their names with the goal of making a greater impact on a national and international audience. Thus did Reginald Dwight become rock composer and singer *Elton John*, Edna Gilhooley become actress *Ellen Burstyn*, and Archibald Leach become longtime star *Cary Grant*.

In addition, some of the psychological studies noted earlier have indicated that desirable or undesirable qualities linked to names may affect our opinions and possibly our actions.

After an experiment involving the grading of essays, researchers found that teachers generally gave higher grades to papers when the student's name aroused a positive response, even though all the essays were supposedly of comparable merit. In another study, children with more popular names seemed to have a stronger self-image and were more consistent in their goals; they also tended to have higher expectations of themselves and achieved higher test scores, while children with less popular names had lower scores. Other researchers have disputed these findings and questioned the methods employed in these studies. They argue that names can't be judged in a vacuum; factors such as the socioeconomic level, sex, and ethnic background of participants must be taken into account in any evaluation.

In a larger sense, it's clear that our impressions ultimately will depend on our reaction to the person. A name is like a calling card: it sets in motion initial vibrations, but we have to meet the individual in order to make a more definitive judgment. The situation may be compared to a blind date. A name we view favorably won't be able to rescue a mismatched encounter, but a name we've never liked before can't possibly stand in the way of love at first sight.

## A Tale of Three Presidents

For a final look at the influence that names may or may not have, consider a tale of three presidents:

Woodrow Wilson was a reserved man, difficult to get to know. He seemed aloof in his dealings with others, especially with members of Congress. Someone remarked of him that things might have been very different if he'd had another name. After all, you couldn't call him *Woody*. (In fact, his first name was *Thomas*, but no one ever called him that either. *Woodrow* was his mother's family name.) More recently, another president routinely used the familiar *Jimmy* in conducting official business, but it didn't seem to help him with Congress or the public. But a president whose actual name was the one-of-the-boys *Harry* had an easy relationship with just about everybody.

Names can be important—and personality even more important.

# 7. Where Our Names Come From

In 1620, when the Pilgrims landed at Plymouth in the *Mayflower*, they brought with them their own naming customs. Most of the parents bore traditional names like *Anne* and *John*, but as members of a Protestant religious group called the Puritans, many of them wanted to put a new stamp on their children's names, which would also be a part of their new life in America. For centuries past among Christians, babies had been named for saints recognized by the Roman Catholic Church. Now, as a result of the Reformation of the 1500s, Protestants rejected many practices of the Catholic Church; some of the new English sects, like the Puritans, also disagreed with principles adopted by the recently established Church of England. New naming patterns offered a symbolic way of demonstrating their adherence to fundamental beliefs.

Names and concepts that were not found in the Holy Scriptures were judged unworthy of consideration. The majority of parents selected well-known Old Testament names like *Esther* and *Rachel*, *Samuel* and *Joshua*. For daughters, they also favored names taken from biblical virtues— *Prudence*, *Mercy*, *Faith*, *Patience*. However, some were even more determined to display their convictions. They picked unusual names like *Meshullemeth* and *Jehoshaphat*; not content with single-word virtues, they favored more elaborate constructions such as *Preserved from Temptation*, *Make Peace with the Lord*, and *Deliverance through Enduring Faith*. For practical reasons, these names were shortened over time to *Preserved*, *Makepeace*, and *Deliverance*.

They encountered another set of naming practices among the native Americans, called Indians since the voyages of discovery by Columbus. Primarily, these parents followed a custom of more primitive times by naming their children after natural phenomena. They might be qualities found in nature and animals (*Running Brook*, *Swift Deer*), events that occurred around the time of childbirth (*Dark Storm Cloud*), or the appearance of the baby (*Smiling Eyes*).

On the surface, these two naming traditions, Puritan and native American, may seem to have nothing in common, but in fact they illustrate some of the underlying reasons for naming that link parents and societies despite a host of geographical, historical, and cultural differences. The Puritans' abstract-virtue names were not unlike the qualities-of-nature names adopted by the native Americans, and even some of the Old Testament names were derived originally from impressions at birth, as with *Naomi* ("pleasant") or *Solomon* ("peaceful"). The native Americans, too, sometimes used name clusters similar to the Puritans' scriptural texts.

Moreover, the two traditions were united by a factor common to all names. Although we are often unaware of it, every name has or had a meaning. Tracing the meaning can not only enhance the parents' experience in giving a name to their child but may also be like a mini-detective story.

Probably the very first names were simply descriptive, based on personal appearance. They were most likely not given by parents at birth but bestowed later on by other members of a tribe as a means of identification. We do the same thing in childhood when we call someone "Red" or "Blondie," and in subsequent years when we use nicknames like "Big *Jim*" or "Little *Mary*." Eventually, these descriptions lost their original meaning and were used as actual names. The Romans, a methodical people, went a step further and institutionalized such names to cover all members of a particular clan. Thus the founder of the *Calvinus* clan must have been bald, for that is the root meaning of *Calvin*.

Naming took on its true cultural significance when it became part of the ritual of childbirth. In addition to describing the baby's appearance, names were also used to express the parents' feelings. The happiness caused by the event is still present in such biblical names as *Miriam* ("longed-for child") and *David* ("beloved"). The Greeks tended to emphasize qualities—for girls, moral or intellectual, as with *Agnes* ("chaste") and *Sophia* ("wisdom"); for boys, dynamic and active, as with *Alexander* ("protector of mankind") and *Nicholas* ("victory of the people").

An expansion of the moral concept brought religion into the naming process. The Greeks and Romans had many epithets—additional names—for their gods and goddesses, because they seldom discarded an old god when a new one was accepted. This provided an ample choice for bestowing the name of a spiritual protector. Among the Hebrew people, whose monotheism was their greatest contribution to civilization, there was no such choice, so they came up with another solution. God was given a number of different names, each with a distinct shade of meaning. Thus the same concept of "gift of

God" or "God's gift" is expressed by three such apparently different names as *Jonathan*, *Nathaniel*, and *Matthew*. They also created many combinations employing the same root. For example, nearly every feminine and masculine name from the Bible that begins with *Jo-* includes "God" in its meaning.

The early Christians, most of whom came from the Hebrew tradition, adopted new types of names—principally Greek and Latin—to emphasize their new identity. Widespread persecution gave them many martyrs who, as saints, were later regarded as role models and heavenly guardians. At first the use of saints' names for children was a Christian custom; later it was officially adopted as church policy. As church and government became intertwined during the Middle Ages, it was also civil policy as well, and remained so for many centuries in Catholic countries.

Another result of the adoption of saints' names was the addition to the available list of hundreds of names from other nations and cultures. Many of these names were brought back to Europe by those who voyaged to the Holy Land and the Middle East in the Crusades that began late in the eleventh century.

Around the same time, another geographic movement, although more limited in scope, had a profound impact on English naming practices. This was the invasion of England by William of Normandy in 1066. The British Isles had already been conquered and colonized several times during the previous thousand years—by the Celts, Romans, Germanic tribes (later the Anglo-Saxons), and Scandinavians. Each wave of invaders had left naming imprints on the islands. The Norman Conquest was not only the last wave but in many ways also the most far-reaching.

The Normans shared many of the same ancestors with

the Britons, whose name indicates that they came originally from Brittany, in France. The Normans' arrival in England reinforced some of the influences that had faded after the earlier colonizations. The basic principle of naming among medieval peoples was to have on hand an extensive pool of word elements that could be combined in a practically unlimited fashion. For example, the name of an animal could be enhanced by adding to it a quality associated with the same creature: *Bernard* is from "bear-courage," *Leonard* from "lion-courage." It didn't matter in many cases which element came first. The two names *Harold* and *Walter* use the same word elements ("army-power") in different order. As usual, names for men chiefly emphasized strength and bravery, while women's names borrowed from virtues: *Adelaide*, a favorite among Germanic groups, is composed of "noble-quality." But force played a role here also, as with *Gertrude* ("spear-strength").

In addition, the Normans brought their own French names, along with some of Latin origin; Latin took on even greater importance, because nearly all official records were kept in this language, giving names from every source a Latin cast. And finally, the Normans created a foundation for future naming by conducting the first genuine census of English landowners and property. The result was known as the "Domesday (or Doomsday) Book," because a final judgment in disputes over property rights was supposed to be based on this written record.

The concept of family names or surnames, which had seldom been used until then except among the Romans, grew out of this census. These second names not only served to identify ancestry but soon became indispensable for legal and tax purposes. By the fifteenth century, family names were found generally throughout England. Among other sources, they were taken from ordinary locations: *Brooke* ("brook"), *Ford* ("crossing"); from physical appearance: *Russell* ("red-haired"), *Grant* ("tall"); from occupations: *Howard* ("chief guardian"), *Piper* ("pipe-player"), *Sherman* ("shearer"); and from villages and place names: *Wesley* ("west meadow"), *Milton* ("mill town"), *Lindsay* ("linden island").

In time, many of these names also became available for use as first names.

This heritage was represented in America by the Pilgrims and by other English, Scottish, and Irish settlers. Colonists from different lands—Spain, Holland, France, and then many others—added new customs and practices, from the eighteenth century down to the present day. Their combined traditions have conferred on the United States probably the greatest storehouse of names of any nation in the world.

# 8. Names for Girls

Variants, pet forms, and diminutives are listed under the major name heading. For a complete list of names, see the index.

## — A —

### Abigail

Hebrew, "source of joy" or "a father's joy." Var: **Abbey, Abbie, Abby, Gael, Gail, Gale, Gayle.**

The earliest recorded reference to this name is in the First Book of Samuel in the Old Testament, describing the woman who became David's wife. It was adopted in England after the Protestant Reformation, when many old names were revived. The shorter forms were *Abbey* and *Abbie*, and though they are still in use, *Gail* and *Gael* are more customary now. The latter may also be derived from the Gaelic language of Ireland and Scotland.

In early American history, Abigail Adams was the wife

of the second president (John) and the mother of the sixth (John Quincy). Perhaps the best-known bearer of the name in our own time is Abigail Van Buren (Pauline Friedman Phillips). As "Dear Abby," she claims 65 million readers around the world for her column of advice.

## Adeline

Old German, "noble quality." Var: **Ada, Adelaide, Adele, Adelia, Adelina, Adelle, Della, Edeline, Heidi, Lina.** See also **Audrey, Ethel.**

In its oldest form as *Adelaide*, the name dates back at least to the tenth century, when it was popular in Germany and France, but it didn't gain attention in England until the accession to the throne of William IV in 1830, whose German-born queen was named Adelaide. Her name was commemorated by streets, buildings, and the capital of South Australia. Around the turn of the century in the United States, the composition of "Sweet Adeline" gave the newly emerging barbershop quartets someone they never stopped singing about. The Swiss novel for children, *Heidi*, demonstrates a short German form. Longer forms are seldom seen today. Nutritionist Adelle Davis; singer Della Reese.

## Agatha

Greek, "good." Var: **Agathe, Agathy, Aggie, Aggy.**
An early Christian martyr, St. Agatha is the patron of Malta and of Catania, Sicily, the site of her tomb. According to legend, her veil is supposed to have preserved the town from destruction by the volcano on Mount Etna. By extension, she became the saint whose protection was invoked against fire. Our own century's most famous *Agatha* is undoubtedly Agatha Christie, prolific mystery writer.

## Agnes

Greek, "chaste." Var: **Aggie, Agnessa, Nessa, Ines, Inez.**

Because her name is related to the Latin word for lamb, a symbol of purity and holiness, St. Agnes of Rome is often depicted holding a baby lamb in her arms. John Keats's "The Eve of St. Agnes" poetically describes the tradition whereby girls tried to visualize their future husbands on the evening before January 21, her name day. The American choreographer Agnes de Mille revolutionized dance in the musical theater beginning with Rodgers and Hammerstein's *Oklahoma!* (1943).

## Alexandra

Greek, "protector of mankind." Var: **Alexa, Alexine, Alexis, Sandi, Sandra, Sandy, Sondra.**

Since Alexander the Great in the fourth century B.C., the name has been a favorite of royal families in both its masculine and feminine forms. Like *Adelaide*, it gained prominence in England in the nineteenth century when a Danish princess named Alexandra married the Prince of Wales, later Edward VII. Many landmarks in London are named after her. Princess Alexandra of Kent is the cousin of Queen Elizabeth. Justice Sandra Day O'Connor is the first woman to serve on the United States Supreme Court. Actress Alexis Smith.

## Alice

Old German, "noble." Var: **Alethea, Ali, Alicia, Alisa, Alissa, Alix, Alyce, Alyse.** See also **Alison.**

A close relative of *Adelaide*, it was shortened to its Latin version, *Alicia*, by the twelfth century, and this and other forms remained popular for many centuries thereafter. However, all were overshadowed by *Alice* after 1865, when *Alice's Adventures in Wonderland* was published. Lewis Carroll named the heroine of this book and its sequel, *Through the Looking Glass*, after Alice Liddell, the daughter of a friend, to whom many of the adventures were first told. Actress Ali MacGraw; novelist Alice Walker.

## Alison

Old German, "noble." Var: **Allison, Alyson.**

This Scottish version of *Alice* became fashionable in this country in the 1950s and '60s, with the decline in popularity of the original. It was the name of a principal character in the successful TV series *Peyton Place*, based on the novel and its movie version.

## Amanda

Latin, "lovable." Var: **Manda, Mandie, Mandy.**

In the latter part of the seventeenth century, the freshness of Restoration drama in England included the creation of bright new character names, especially for women. Most of them had a Latin root. *Amanda* made its first appearance in this way, later turning up in romantic poetry and novels. It is also the mother's name in a key work of the modern American theater, Tennessee Williams' *The Glass Menagerie*.

## Amelia

Old German, "industrious." Var: **Amalia, Amalie, Amelie, Ameline.**

See **Emily**. The story of Amelia Earhart, the first woman pilot to fly the Atlantic, is still a fascinating one. She vanished mysteriously on a Pacific flight in 1937.

## Amy

French, "beloved." Var: **Aimee, Amie.**

A favorite in the nineteenth century, this name appears in the American classics *Little Women* and *The Adventures of Tom Sawyer*. Amy Lowell was awarded the Pulitzer Prize for poetry in 1926. Golf champion Amy Alcott.

## Anastasia

Greek "resurrection." Var: **Stacey, Stacie, Stacy.**

A familiar name among early Christians, it spread to Western Europe and later to Russia, where it won the greatest favor. The possibility that the czar's daughter of that name escaped death after the Russian Revolution is a perennial subject of speculation. The shorter forms are popular here and in England.

## Andrea

Greek, "womanly." Var: **Andree, Andria, Andriana, Andy.**

The masculine form of the name, *Andrew*, has always been more widely adopted, but the feminine version is now gaining popularity. Tennis star Andrea Jaeger.

## Angela

Greek, "messenger." Var: **Angele, Angelica, Angelina, Angeline, Angelita, Angelique, Angie.**

Angels were so designated because they were viewed as God's messengers. The name was fashionable until the Reformation, when it was dropped by the Puritans along with specific angel names like Gabriel and Michael. Its revival began toward the end of the eighteenth century. Actresses Angela Lansbury, Angie Dickinson.

## Annabel

Latin, "lovable." Var: **Annabella, Annabelle.**

It would seem logical to view this name as a combination of *Anne* (see below) and *Belle* or *Bella* ("beautiful"), and undoubtedly some parents have adopted it with this combination in mind. However, it probably originated as *Amabel*, a Latin name that gave rise to *Mabel* and possibly to *Arabella*. Edgar Allan Poe's poem "Annabel Lee" brought it new popularity in the nineteenth century.

## Anne

Hebrew, "grace." Var: **Ana, Anita, Ann, Anna, Annette, Annice, Annick, Annie, Annika, Annine, Anya.** See also **Hannah, Marianne, Nancy, Nina.**

The origin of this traditional favorite can be traced to Hannah, mother of the prophet Samuel in the Old Testament. (According to tradition, St. Anna or Anne was the mother of the Virgin Mary, but she is not mentioned directly in the Scriptures.)

It was as *Anna*, the Greek and Latin form, that the name appeared in Europe, changing to *Anne* around the thirteenth century, first in France and then in England, where it has been the name of six queens. The preferred form in Russia remained *Anna*, and one of the best-known heroines in literature is Tolstoy's *Anna Karenina*. Other books and plays have included *Anna Christie* by Eugene O'Neill, *Anna and the King of Siam* (which became *The King and I*), and the *Diary of Anne Frank*. The musical *Annie* is the most recent example, and this version of the name seems to be returning to popularity.

For at least two hundred years, *Anne* has also been used in a combined form, most often with *Mary* but with many other names as well.

## Antonia

Latin, "beyond price." Var: **Antoinette, Netta, Netty, Toni, Tonia, Tony.**

The feminine version of this Roman clan name is most familiar now in its shorter forms, perhaps in part because of the annual Tony awards, the Broadway theater's equivalent of Hollywood's Oscar. The awards are named for producer and director Antoinette Perry.

## April

Latin, "to open." Var: **Averil, Avril.**

Some authorities link the derivation of the month of April to Aphrodite, the Greek goddess of love; the two words may have a common origin. Among the names of months, only those of spring have achieved any degree of popularity (a fairly recent development). *June* has been adopted most widely. *May* was used in the nineteenth century, but often as an abbreviation of *Mary*.

## Arlene

Irish, "a pledge." Var: **Arlena, Arleen, Arlen, Arlina, Arline, Arlyn.**

This name is assumed to be Gaelic, with the root shown above, because the sound of the ending is similar to that of so many other Irish names (*Colleen, Eileen, Maureen*). Beyond that, its history is uncertain. It achieved some degree of success in this country in the early 1900s, but it hasn't yet benefited from the Irish revival. Actress Arlene Dahl.

## Ashley

Old English, "ash tree meadow." Var: **Ashlee, Ashly.**

An example of the way a name can evolve from place

name to family name to masculine first name to feminine name. Perhaps the best-known *Ashley* is a male character, Ashley Wilkes, in Margaret Mitchell's *Gone With the Wind*, published in 1936. Today the name is almost exclusively feminine.

### Audrey

Old English, "noble strength." Var: **Audra, Audrie, Audrye.** See also **Adeline, Ethel.**

*Audrey* comes from the same Old German root as *Adeline*, with an English variation. It started as the short form of the name of an early saint, Etheldreda, but by the sixteenth century it stood by itself. The name only became fashionable in the late nineteenth century. Actress Audrey Hepburn.

## — B —

### Barbara

Greek, "foreign, strange." Var: **Babette, Babs, Barbie, Barbra, Bobbie.**

According to legend, St. Barbara was an early Christian martyr whose veneration was widely established by the ninth century; many generations of daughters were named for her. Probably for this reason, the popularity of the name declined after the Protestant Reformation, then gradually returned to favor. "Barbara Allen" is one of the oldest and most familiar English ballads. In modern times it has been the name of many leading actresses, among them Barbra Streisand, Barbara Stanwyck, Barbara Bel Geddes. Television commentator Barbara Walters.

## Beatrice

Latin, "bringer of joy." Var: **Bea, Beatrix, Bee, Trix, Trixie.**

This very old name has survived at least partly because of its many echoes in English literature, including the heroines of Shakespeare's *Much Ado About Nothing* and Thackeray's *Henry Esmond* (Beatrix), and the author of the children's classic *Peter Rabbit* (Beatrix Potter). But the most famous bearer of the name is Italian: Dante's guide to Paradise in *The Divine Comedy*.

## Belinda

Spanish, "beautiful." Var: **Bella, Linda.**

While it existed elsewhere in different forms, the name was apparently unknown in England until the late seventeenth century, when it appeared in Restoration drama along with other new names (see **Amanda**). It made an even greater impression as the name of the heroine of Alexander Pope's poetic satire "The Rape of the Lock," and its subsequent popularity is usually credited to him.

## Beth

Hebrew, "house." Var: see **Elizabeth.**

A short form of *Elizabeth*, this name has a second identity derived from another Hebrew source, the word for house or home, and is popular by itself. Beth was one of the four sisters in Louisa May Alcott's *Little Women*. Playwright Beth Henley won the Pulitzer Prize in 1981.

## Beverly

Old English, "beaver's meadow." Var: **Bev, Beverlee, Bevie.**

Like *Ashley*, this is another illustration of a formerly

masculine name, used mainly in England, that is now
feminine. Opera star Beverly Sills.

## Bianca

Italian, "white." Var: **Blanca, Blanche.**

Although *Bianca* appears in two Shakespearean plays,
*Othello* and *The Taming of the Shrew*, it is usually seen
here and in England in its French form, *Blanche*. Now
the Italian form is becoming more prominent, perhaps in
part because of Bianca Jagger, former wife of rock star
Mick Jagger.

## Bonnie

Latin, "good." Var: **Bonita, Bonny, Bunny.**

Despite its Latin roots, *Bonnie* comes more directly
from a Scottish word whose shades of meaning range
from "charming" and "lovely" to "excellent." The film
*Bonnie and Clyde* brought the name to a wide audience.
Actress Bonnie Franklin.

## Bridget

Irish, "strength." Var: **Biddy, Birgit, Birgitta, Bride,
Bridey, Brigette, Brigid, Brigida, Brigit, Brigita, Brigitte, Gitta, Gitte.**

Along with Patrick and Columba, Bridget of Kildare
is one of the three great saints of Ireland. Born in the
fifth century, she is said to have founded four monasteries
and lived a life of great religious dedication. In the fourteenth century, a Swedish namesake established an order
of nuns known as the Brigittines. Opera and concert star
Birgit Nilsson; actress Brigitte Bardot; author Brigid
Brophy.

**Brooke**

Old English, "brook, stream." Var: **Brook, Brooks.**

In the past this name was used about equally (but never widely) in its masculine and feminine forms; now it is preferred as a name for girls. Actress-model Brooke Shields; philanthropist Brooke Astor.

— C —

**Camilla**

Latin, "attendant." Var: **Camella, Camille, Millie, Milly.**

It derives originally from a term designating attendants in Roman religious ceremonies. In the nineteenth century it gained its greatest fame as a result of the novel and play by Dumas, *Lady of the Camellias*, which served as the basis for Verdi's opera *La Traviata* and, still later, for one of Greta Garbo's memorable film roles, *Camille*. It is a pet name and not the given name of the heroine, and the Latin root has no relation to the flower that is her symbol. The flower was named for Georg Josef Kamel, who first described it in the eighteenth century.

**Candace**

Greek, "glowing white." Var: **Candee, Candice, Candie, Candy, Kandace, Kandi, Kandy.**

The formal title of ancient Ethiopian queens, it later became combined with Greek and Latin words for whiteness, possibly because of the association with royal garments. Actress Candice Bergen.

## Carmen

Latin, "song." Var: **Carmencita, Carmina, Carmine, Carmita, Charmaine.**

An alternative origin of this popular name is from *Santa Maria del Carmen*, referring to Mount Carmel in Israel and the Carmelite order founded in the Middle Ages. As with *Dolores*, it was used originally as a substitute for the name of the mother of Jesus. The most famous fictional bearer of the name is the chief character in Georges Bizet's opera *Carmen* (1875), from a novel by the French author Prosper Merimée.

## Carol

Old German, "man." Var: **Carla, Carlene, Carly, Carola, Carole, Carolina, Caroline, Carolyn, Carrie, Carroll, Caryl, Karla, Karole.** See also **Charlotte.**

The feminine form of *Carl* and *Charles* has been a favorite name in Europe since the sixteenth century. It seems likely that the most popular early forms in England were *Caroline* and *Carolina*. These names, as well as the Carolina colonies in America, honored the newly crowned King Charles II and the Restoration of the royal House of Stuart in 1660. *Caroline* became even more fashionable when George II succeeded to the throne in the early eighteenth century; Caroline was the name of his queen. The shorter *Carol* and *Carole* weren't introduced until the 1900s. *Carrie*, a pet form in the late nineteenth century, was recently revived as a name in its own right.

Princess Caroline of Monaco; actress Carrie Fisher; singers Carole King, Carly Simon. Theodore Dreiser's novel *Sister Carrie* (1900).

## Catherine

Greek, "pure." Var: **Caitlin, Cassie, Catalina, Catarina, Caterina, Catharine, Cathie, Cathleen, Cathryn, Cathy.**

See **Katharine.** This spelling apparently began as a French form. It was the more popular of the two in the United States in the nineteenth and early twentieth centuries, but it has had a decline since then.

## Cecilia

Latin, "blind." Var: **Cecile, Cecily, Celia, Cicely, Cicily, Cissie, Cissy.** See also **Sheila.**

From the name of an old Roman clan, whose founder possibly was sightless. The most famous Cecilia was a reported third-century saint who later became the patron of music, especially church music. The name was popular throughout the Middle Ages, fell off with the Protestant Reformation of the sixteenth century, and then took on new life in eighteenth-century literature. Actress Cicely Tyson.

## Charity

Latin, "love, affection." Var: **Cara, Charissa, Charita, Cher, Cherry.**

The most important commandments to Christians were to love God and to love one another, and this was the original meaning of the word and the name. Gradually it acquired the meaning of being generous in assisting others, thus demonstrating one's love. It was brought to America by the Pilgrims, who frequently named their daughters after the three virtues Faith, Hope, and Charity.

## Charlotte

Old German, "man." Var: **Carlita, Carlota, Carlotta, Charleen, Charlene, Charlotta, Cher, Cheryl, Lola, Lolita, Lotte, Lottie, Lotty, Sharyl, Sharleen, Sharlene, Sheryl.**

See **Carol**. This French and English feminine form of *Charles* was probably the first version to become established in England, around the mid-seventeenth century, but it became popular only one hundred years later, when George III took Charlotte of Mecklenburg as his queen. (Her predecessor was named Caroline.) He was the king against whom the American colonists launched the Revolutionary War. Charlotte Brontë, author of the classic *Jane Eyre* (1847) and other novels.

## Christina

Latin, "follower of Christ." Var: **Chris, Chrissie, Chrissy, Christiana, Christiane, Christine, Teena, Tina.** See also **Kristin.**

From a Greek word used in the translation of the Old Testament for the Hebrew *messiah*, or "chosen one." An early bearer of the name was a martyr in Rome, and many Italian Christians gave her name to their daughters. It reached Britain from Italy in about the twelfth century and has remained popular ever since. Tennis champion Chris Evert Lloyd.

## Clare

Latin, "bright." Var: **Clair, Claire, Clara, Clarabelle, Claretta, Claribel, Clarice, Clarinda, Clarissa, Clarita.**

In various forms this name has been in wide use since the thirteenth century, when it became well known in connection with Clare of Assisi, who founded with St. Francis the order of nuns called the Poor Clares. It was later given a number of poetic variations, as in *Clarissa Harlowe* (1748), the title character of an early novel by Samuel Richardson, whose *Pamela* was also responsible for that name's success.

A famous namesake two centuries later was Clarissa Harlowe Barton, organizer of the American Red Cross. She was known as *Clara*, a revival of the Latin form that was fashionable in the nineteenth century. The variation most recently popular has been the French *Claire*. Both *Clare* and *Clair* have also been used occasionally for boys but are seldom given today. There was a masculine St. Clair in the Middle Ages, but the name may also be taken from County Clare, Ireland. Author and political figure Clare Boothe Luce; actress Claire Bloom.

## Colette

Greek, "victory of the people." Var: **Coletta, Collette.** See **Nicole**. Colette was the pen name of a French novelist, Sidonie Gabrielle Claudine Colette, author of the book that served as the basis for the film *Gigi*, Academy Award-winner in 1958.

## Colleen

Irish, "girl." Var: **Colline.**
The Irish word for a young woman used specifically as a name. Novelist Colleen McCullough; actress Colleen Dewhurst.

## Constance

Latin, "consistency, perseverance." Var: **Connie, Constantia, Constantina, Constantine, Constanza.**
When the Emperor Constantine allowed the practice

of Christianity in the Roman Empire early in the fourth century, both the masculine and feminine forms of the name immediately became popular among Christian families. Until the Reformation, *Constantia* was the preferred version for girls; it dropped from favor and was eventually replaced by *Constance*. Singer Connie Francis; actress Connie Stevens.

## Courtney

French, "from Courtenay." Var: **Courtnay.**
Like *Ashley* and others, this old place name (also a town in British Columbia) was formerly a family name and masculine first name; it has only recently been adopted for girls. The French word means "short nose."

## Crystal

Greek, "ice, crystal." Var: **Chrystal, Kristal.**
Like other jewel names (*Amber*, *Beryl*), it came into fashion in the late nineteenth century. Currently it seems to be having a revival. Singer Crystal Gayle.

## Cynthia

Latin, "from Cynthus." Var: **Cindie, Cindy, Cynthie, Cynthy.**
See **Diana**. Cynthia is another name for the goddess of the hunt and the moon, known to the Romans as Diana and to the Greeks as Artemis. She was supposedly born on Mount Cynthus on the Aegean island of Delos.

# ___ D ___

## Daisy

Old English, "day's eye." Var: **Daisie, Daysie.**
The daisy, a symbol of the sun, has traditionally oc-
cupied a special place among flowers. The name was
adopted in England and the United States in the 1800s.
Judith Krantz's novel *Princess Daisy*; Daisy Buchanan
in *The Great Gatsby* by F. Scott Fitzgerald.

## Dana

Scandinavian, "from Denmark." Var: **Dane, Danica.**
More frequently a masculine name but occasionally
used for girls. Actress Dana Wynter.

## Danielle

Hebrew, "God is my judge." Var: **Danella, Daniela,
Daniele, Dany.**
This French feminine form of *Daniel*, an old biblical
name that was frequently found among the Puritans, has
been one of the most popular American names in recent
years. Novelist Danielle Steele.

## Dawn

Old English, "daybreak." Var: **Dawna, Dawne.**
Introduced about one hundred years ago and still a
favorite. Actress Dawn Addams.

## Deborah

Hebrew, "bee." Var: **Deb, Debbie, Debby, Debora, Debra, Devorah.**

An early name in the Old Testament. The most famous Deborah appears in the Book of Judges, a prophetess and judge who helped to free the Israelites from the domination of the king of Canaan. The "Song of Deborah" celebrating the victory is one of the oldest biblical poems. The Puritans revived the name in the seventeenth century. Actresses Deborah Kerr, Debbie Reynolds.

## Deirdre

Irish, "sorrow." Var: **Dedee, Dee, Deirdra, Didi.**

A number of other roots of the name have been suggested, but in view of the tragic nature of her legend, involving her lover's untimely death and then her own, this one seems the most likely. The legend was retold in dramatic form by Irish writers William Butler Yeats (*Deirdre*) and J. M. Synge (*Deirdre of the Sorrows*) early in this century, when the name became popular. Like other old Celtic names, it is being adopted more widely today.

## Diana

Latin, "divine." Var: **Deanna, Deanne, Di, Diahann, Diane, Dianna, Dianne, Dyan.** See also **Cynthia.**

Diana was the name given to the Roman goddess of the hunt and the moon, roughly equivalent to the Greek Artemis. She was also known as Cynthia, Delia, and Phoebe, among other names. Her temple at Ephesus, in what is now Turkey, was one of the seven wonders of the ancient world. The name appeared in Europe in the late fifteenth century, first in France (as *Diane*), and subsequently in England, where it became popular in the mid-eighteenth century.

Princess Diana, wife of Prince Charles, heir to the English throne; actresses Diahann Carroll, Dyan Cannon; San Francisco mayor Dianne Feinstein.

## Dolores

Spanish, "sorrows." Var: **Delora, Delores, Dolly, Dolorita, Lola, Lolita.**

For many centuries the name of the mother of Jesus was considered by Christians to be too sacred to be used in naming, particularly in Spanish-speaking countries. And so the name was bestowed in indirect ways, for example as *Dolores*, from *Santa Maria de los Dolores* (St. Mary of the Sorrows). In paintings Mary is sometimes shown with her heart pierced by seven swords, representing seven sorrowful events connected with the life of her son.

## Donna

Italian, "lady." Var: **Dona, Donella, Donia.**

*Domina*, the Latin word for lady, is *donna* in Italian and *dona* in Spanish. It came into use as a name in English only in this century. Singer Donna Summers.

## Doris

Greek, "a Dorian woman." Var: **Dori, Doria, Dorice, Dorise, Dorita, Dory.**

The Dorians were an ancient Greek tribe. In Greek mythology, Doris was the wife of Nereus, god of the Aegean Sea, and the mother of fifty sea nymphs called the Nereids. The name was introduced in England late in the sixteenth century. Actress Doris Day.

## Dorothy

Greek, "gift of God." Var: **Dodie, Dody, Dolly, Dora, Dorinda, Dorothea, Dorothee, Dot, Dotty, Thea, Theodora, Feodora.**

In its first appearance as a name, it was *Theodora*, but over time the two elements were reversed. It appeared in Elizabethan England as *Doll*, and by the eighteenth century this form was so popular that it was a slang term for women generally, as well as for a girl's favorite toy. Dorothea (Dolley) Madison was the wife of the fourth president. Probably the most famous Dorothy throughout the world is the heroine of the book and film classic *The Wizard of Oz*. Skating star Dorothy Hamill.

# — E —

## Edith

Old English, "rich gift." Var: **Eda, Edie, Edyth, Edythe, Eydie.**

An old name that practically disappeared in England after the Norman Conquest of the eleventh century, later revived by the Victorians. Singers Edith Piaf, Edie Adams, Eydie Gorme.

## Edna

Hebrew, "rejuvenation." Var: **Eddy, Edie.**

It gained favor in the United States in the late nineteenth century, then declined in popularity. Poet Edna St. Vincent Millay and novelist Edna Ferber both won Pulitzer Prizes (in 1923 and 1925).

**Eileen**

Irish, "bringer of light." Var: **Aileen.**
See **Helen**. *My Sister Eileen*, a collection of stories
by Ruth McKenney, has served as the basis for a play,
a musical, and two movies.

**Elaine**

Old French, "light." Var: **Alaine, Elaina, Elane,
Elayne, Ellen, Ellin, Ellyn.**
See **Helen**. This French form of a favorite name
gained attention with the publication of Tennyson's
*Idylls of the King* in 1859, a retelling of the Camelot
legend that includes the romance of Lancelot and Elaine.
Movie and stage director Elaine May; actress Ellen
Burstyn.

**Eleanor**

Old French, "bright one." Var: **El, Eleanora, Elea-
nore, Elinor, Elinore, Ella, Ellie, Lenora, Lenore,
Leonore, Nell, Nellie, Nelly, Nora.**
See **Helen**. Another version of the name that achieved
wide popularity because of Eleanor of Aquitaine, a queen
of England who died in the early thirteenth century. For
a long period it was more fashionable than the original.
The name of the wife of President Franklin D. Roosevelt.
Nellie Tayloe Ross, first woman elected governor in the
United States (Wyoming, 1924).

**Elizabeth**

Hebrew, "God's oath." Var: **Babette, Belita, Bess,
Bessie, Betsy, Bett, Betta, Bette, Bettina, Betty, Elisa,
Elisabeth, Elise, Elissa, Eliza, Elsa, Elsbeth, Else,
Elsie, Elspeth, Elyse, Ilsa, Ilse, Libby, Lisabeth, Lis-**

**beth, Lizabeth.** See also **Beth, Isabel, Liza.**

The many variations of this name provide evidence of its enduring appeal. It was the name of the mother of John the Baptist in the New Testament, who was also related to the mother of Jesus, and of four other saints. It has also graced many queens, among them Elizabeth of Hungary, a thirteenth-century monarch who devoted her life to helping the poor. Best known of all is probably Elizabeth I of England; her reign in the sixteenth century was remarkable for the great vitality demonstrated in exploration, trade, architecture, and literature, with many poets and authors, including Shakespeare, dedicating their works to her. The current Elizabeth is only the second English queen to bear the name.

Elizabeth Cady Stanton, a nineteenth-century United States pioneer in the women's rights movement. Elizabeth Ann Seton, first American-born saint, canonized in 1975.

## Emily

Old German, "industrious." Var: **Em, Emelina, Emeline, Emilia, Emilie, Emiline, Emlynne, Emmie, Emmy, Millie, Milly.** See also **Amelia.**

The feminine version of *Emil*. Some researchers trace it back still further to a Latin clan name, *Aemilius*. It reached a peak in the nineteenth century with such celebrated namesakes as Emily Brontë, author of *Wuthering Heights*, and the American poet Emily Dickinson.

## Emma

Old German, "universal." Var: **Em, Ema, Emmie, Emmy.**

Although similar to *Emily*, it has a different root; it may also be related to the Old German word for nurse. It was given to two memorable literary characters, Flaubert's *Madame Bovary* and Jane Austen's *Emma*. Television's annual Emmy awards are named not for a person but for the image orthicon tube ("immy") used for transmission of pictures in the television camera. In 1821, Emma Willard founded the first American college for women, now a boarding school for girls in Troy, New York.

## Erica

Scandinavian, "ruler." Var: **Erika.**

The feminine form of *Eric* has only recently come into popular use for girls in the United States. It is also the name for plants of the heath or heather variety. Novelist Erica Jong.

## Erin

Irish, "Ireland." Var: **Erina, Erinne.**

Another Irish name that has gained wider attention. The St. Patrick's Day (March 17) slogan *Erin go bragh!* means "Ireland forever!" Actress Erin Moran.

## Estelle

Latin, "star." Var: **Estele, Estella, Estrella, Estrellita, Stella.**

See **Esther.** The Latin form, *Stella*, is usually credited to the eighteenth-century satirist Jonathan Swift (*Gulliver's Travels*), who gave it as a pet name to a young woman with whom he fell in love; her real name was Esther. However, it was apparently invented more than a century earlier by an Elizabethan poet, Sir Philip Sidney, but Swift's *Journal to Stella* made it famous (see also **Vanessa**). *Estella* became fashionable in the nineteenth century after Charles Dickens used it in his *Great Expectations*.

### Esther

Persian, "star." Var: **Essie, Ester, Ettie, Etty, Hester, Hettie, Hetty.** See also **Estelle.**

The name first appears in the Old Testament in the Book of Esther; she was originally called *Hadassah*, the Hebrew word for the myrtle plant. During the captivity of the Jews in Persia, she was chosen by King Ahasuerus to be his queen and given the Persian name for star, a variation of Ishtar, the Babylonian goddess of love and fertility. She saved the Jews from destruction by Haman, the king's prime minister, an achievement commemorated by the feast of Purim. *Esther* was favored by the Puritans, along with other Old Testament names.

### Ethel

Old English, "noble." Var: **Ethelda, Etheline, Ethelyn.** See also **Adeline, Audrey.**

The name was always used in a combined form (*Etheldreda, Ethelinda*) in the Middle Ages, but it gradually became separated from these other elements. It was very popular in the Victorian era. Actresses Ethel Barrymore, Ethel Merman.

### Eve

Hebrew, "life." Var: **Ava, Ev, Eva, Evie, Evita, Evy.** See also **Evelyn, Zoe.**

The first woman, "mother of all the living," as described in the Book of Genesis. The name appeared initially in Ireland as *Eve* in the eleventh or twelfth century, then reached England, where its preferred form during and after the Middle Ages was *Eva*. By the 1800s it was seldom in use, but the publication in 1852 of Harriet Beecher Stowe's *Uncle Tom's Cabin*, with the character of Little Eva, followed by the immensely popular theatrical version, contributed strongly to the name's revival. It's a curious footnote that Little Eva was actually *Evangeline*, which has nothing to do with *Eve* but comes from the Greek, "bringer of good news," a term originally applied to the four authors of the Christian Gospels. It was then very much in fashion because of Henry Wadsworth Longfellow's poem of the same name, which had appeared only a few years earlier.

The film *All About Eve* won the Academy Award in 1950. More recently the musical *Evita*, based on the life of Argentina's Eva Peron, brought the name new attention.

## Evelyn

Irish, "lively, pleasant." Var: **Ev, Eveleen, Evelin, Evelina, Eveline, Evlyn.**

A name with at least three possible origins. The first is simply one of the Irish forms of *Eve*. The second, given above, is from a similar word related to *Eve*. The third and completely different possibility is based on the French word for hazelnut (*aveline*), brought to England as a name by the Normans in the eleventh century. Beginning in the late seventeenth century, *Evelyn* was given to both boys and girls in England, but now it is a feminine name again. Olympic track champion Evelyn Ashford.

## — F —

## Faith

Latin, "trust, belief." Var: **Fay, Faye, Fayette, Fayth, Fidelia.**

The personification of this virtue goes far back in

history. Fides was an ancient Roman goddess representing faith and trust. The early Christians, borrowing from the Hebrew tradition, transferred this concept specifically to belief in God. The Apostle Paul described faith, hope, and charity (love) as the three great virtues. A French martyr of this name had a devoted following in France and England during the Middle Ages. It was revived by the Puritans after the Reformation, not as a saint's name but as one of the prized virtues. Faith Baldwin was a popular author early in this century.

*Fay* and similar variants may also be related to an Old English and French word for fairy. Actress Faye Dunaway.

## Felicia

Latin, "happy." Var: **Felice, Feliciana, Felicie, Felicity, Felise, Felisse.**

Currently the preferred version of another Puritan virtue name, *Felicity*, derived originally from the name of the Roman goddess of happiness. The feminine form of *Felix*, it is sometimes mistakenly assumed to be a variant of *Phyllis*, which has a different root. Actress Felicia Farr.

## Fiona

Irish, "fair, white." Var: **Fenella, Finella, Fione, Fionna, Fionnula.**

Irish names with this root, similar to *Gwen* in Welsh, are familiar in legend and history, but this particular version was apparently created by William Sharp, a nineteenth-century author of Celtic tales. It has shown growing popularity here and in England.

## Flora

Latin, "flower." Var: **Fiora, Fleur, Flo, Florie, Florrie.** See also **Florence.**

The Roman goddess of flowers and gardens. Her festival corresponded approximately to the celebration of spring later known as May Day, a time for gathering flowers and choosing a May queen.

## Florence

Latin, "flowering, blooming." Var: **Flo, Florance, Florencia, Florentia, Florenz, Florenza, Floretta, Florie, Florrie, Floss, Flossie.**

A name that is possibly a thousand years old, it was given to girls and boys alike through the Middle Ages. Although this dual use became increasingly rare, it persisted until fairly recent times, as illustrated by the name of Florenz Ziegfeld, the famous theatrical producer. However, after the mid-nineteenth century it was almost exclusively a feminine name as a tribute to Florence Nightingale, a symbol of comfort to the sick and wounded and a pioneer in nursing education. She was born in Italy to English parents and was named after the city of her birth.

## Frances

Latin, "from France." Var: **Fan, Fanchette, Fanchon, Fancy, Fannie, Fanny, Fanya, Fran, France, Francey, Francie, Francesca, Francina, Francine, Francisca, Françoise, Frannie, Franny, Frankie.**

Both the masculine and feminine versions of this name spread through Italy and then Europe in the thirteenth and fourteenth centuries, honoring the life of Francis of Assisi (see **Francis**). *Francesca* was the first popular feminine form. The name arrived late in England, where the masculine spelling *Francis* was used for both boys and girls in the sixteenth century. Two hundred years later *Fanny* was the fashionable version. In the United States, *Frances* remained one of the most frequently chosen names until the 1950s; now the Italian *Francesca* seems to be returning to popularity.

Frances Xavier Cabrini (Mother Cabrini), founder of schools and hospitals, was the first United States citizen to be canonized (1946). Frances Perkins, secretary of labor under President Franklin D. Roosevelt, was the first woman member of the Cabinet.

## — G —

### Gabrielle

Hebrew, "woman of God." Var: **Gabi, Gabriela, Gabriele, Gabriella, Gaby, Gavrila.**

The feminine form of *Gabriel*, taken from the name of the archangel who appears in both the Old and New Testaments. A name given more often in French than in English.

### Georgia

Greek, "farmer." Var: **Georgeanne, Georgette, Georgiana, Georgie, Georgina, Georgine, Georgy, Gina, Giorgia.**

Seldom used in England as a name for boys or girls until the Georgian period began in 1714 with King George I. Georgia, last of the original thirteen colonies, was settled during this time. Artist Georgia O'Keeffe.

## Geraldine

Old German, "spear ruler." Var: **Dina, Geraldina, Gerri, Gerrie, Gerry, Jere, Jeri, Jerrie, Jerry.**

Although the masculine form of this name was known in England since the Norman invasion, the feminine version seems to have been created by Henry Howard, a sixteenth-century poet, as a pet name for Lady Elizabeth Fitzgerald. But the name only became popular three centuries later, when a more celebrated poet, Samuel Taylor Coleridge, gave it to a character in his *Christabel*. The form *Jeri* was popular in this country in the post-World War II period. In 1984, Congresswoman Geraldine A. Ferraro of New York, a Democrat, became the first woman to be selected as a candidate for vice-president by a major political party.

## Gillian

Latin, "downy hair." Var: **Gill, Gillie, Jill, Jilly.**

See **Juliana**, of which this was a popular variant in medieval England. Because the hair of youth is soft and downy, some researchers suggest that the meaning gradually became "youthful." The nursery rhyme about Jack and Jill is only one of many examples of the use of the two names for a young man and woman. Actress Jill St. John.

## Ginger

Latin, "ginger plant." Var: **Ginette, Ginnie, Ginny.**

Usually given as a form of *Virginia*, this name also has its own identity traced to the spicy plant. It can sometimes mean "redheaded," although ginger is more yellowish brown than red. Actress Ginger Rogers.

## Giselle

Old German, "a pledge." Var: **Gisela, Gisele, Gizela.**
Still fairly uncommon in the United States and England but well known in France. The romantic ballet *Giselle*, first performed in the mid-nineteenth century, has gained a permanent place in the world of dance.

## Gloria

Latin, "glory." Var: **Glora, Glori, Gloriana, Glorianne, Glory.**
It became fashionable in the last century and reached a peak in the 1940s, although it still retains some popularity. Fashion designer Gloria Vanderbilt; author Gloria Steinem.

## Golda

Old English, "of gold." Var: **Gilda, Goldie, Goldy.**
An old name that periodically returns to favor. Former Israeli prime minister Golda Meir; actress Goldie Hawn.

## Grace

Latin, "grace." Var: **Gracia, Gracie, Grayce, Grazia, Graziella.**
The Graces of mythology, usually three in number, were personifications of charm and beauty. The Christian concept of grace was different: the love of God freely granted to sinners. The Puritans emphasized this aspect in choosing it as a virtue name. Actress Grace Kelly became the princess of Monaco.

## Gwendolen

Welsh, "white circle." Var: **Gwen, Gwendaline, Gwendoline, Gwendolyn, Gwenith, Gwenn, Gwen-**

**nie, Gwyn, Wendie, Wendy.**

The circle in this name's Welsh root is probably a reference to the moon. In the King Arthur legend, Gwendolen was an early love who tried to poison Arthur to prevent him from leaving her; she failed and vanished. The name of Guinevere, Arthur's queen, has a slightly different origin (see **Jennifer**). The shorter forms *Gwen* and *Wendy* are popular today. Poet Gwendolyn Brooks, the first black American to win a Pulitzer Prize (1950).

## — H —

### Hannah

Hebrew, "grace." Var: **Hana, Hanna, Hanni, Hannie.**

See **Anne.** As described in the First Book of Samuel, Hannah was the wife of Elkanah and a woman of deep religious conviction; unable to conceive, she prayed for the gift of a child. When her prayers were answered, she promised to dedicate the child to God's service. He became Samuel, judge and prophet of Israel. For many centuries the Greek and Latin *Anna*, later *Anne*, was the most fashionable form, but in recent years *Hannah* has been revived.

### Harriet

Old German, "ruler of the home." Var: **Etta, Ettie, Hariette, Harrie, Hattie, Hatty, Henrietta, Henriette, Hetty, Nettie, Netty.**

While *Henry* was the name of a series of English kings, the feminine version was rare in England until the early seventeenth century. It was introduced by Henriette Marie, the French wife of Charles I. Trying to pronounce her name in the French style, the English called her *Harriet*. This form remained more popular than the original until the Victorian era, when *Henrietta* was favored. A famous bearer of the name was nineteenth-century American author Harriet Beecher Stowe (*Uncle Tom's Cabin*, 1852).

## Hayley

Old English, "high meadow." Var: **Haley, Halie.**
A place name that evolved into a family name. It has gained prominence as a feminine first name due mainly to the actress Hayley Mills.

## Heather

Middle English, "heath plant." Var: **Heath.** See also **Erica.**
One of the plant and flower names that came into fashion toward the end of the nineteenth century. It has had a strong revival in the past ten years. Actress Heather Menzies.

## Helen

Greek, "bright one." Var: **Helayne, Helena, Helene, Helina, Hella, Ilona, Ilonna.** See also **Eileen, Elaine, Eleanor.**
Many famous women have had this name, but the two best known were very different and lived some fifteen centuries apart.
The first was Helen of Troy, actually the queen of Sparta in Greece and the wife of Menelaus. The most beautiful woman of her time, she was carried off by Paris, a prince of Troy. When he refused to comply with demands by Menelaus for her return, the Greeks launched the Trojan War early in the twelfth century B.C. After a

long siege, they finally entered the city concealed in a wooden horse. The war ended with the total defeat of Troy. Helen was reconciled with Menelaus and returned to Sparta. The last part of the war is described by Homer in the *Iliad*.

The second celebrated name-bearer was Helena, mother of the Roman emperor Constantine. A Christian who was later canonized, she was an important influence in the change of policy that led to the Edict of Milan in A.D. 313, ending the Roman persecution of the Christian church. Veneration of Helena was responsible for the steady growth of the name in the Middle Ages. In a similar fashion, the life of American author Helen Keller, whose early years are dramatized in the play and movie *The Miracle Worker*, has been an inspiration to many.

## Hilary

Latin, "cheerful." Var: **Alair, Hilaire, Hillary.**

An early Christian name, called *Hilaria* in England and *Hilaire* in France, where it was the name of a fourth-century bishop. By the 1500s it was primarily a name for boys, but early in this century it was adopted as a girl's name.

## Hollis

Old English, "holly grove." Var: **Hollie, Holly, Hollye.**

A plant or shrub with red berries traditionally used as a Christmas decoration. Golf champion Hollis Stacy.

## Honor

Latin, "integrity, reputation." Var: **Honora, Honoria, Honorine, Nora, Norine.**

A virtue name made popular by the Puritans. It dates

originally from the thirteenth century, when it was given
equally to girls and boys. Actress Honor Blackman; author Nora Ephron.

### Hope

Old English, "expectation, belief." Var: see **Nadine.**
In Greek mythology, Pandora was the first mortal
woman. She received a beautifully finished box from
Zeus, king of the gods, who warned her never to open
it. Despite the warning, she and her husband looked in-
side. At that moment all the evils of humanity were
released into the world. Only one redeeming quality remained: hope, called Elpis in Greek. The second in the
trio of names *Faith*, *Hope*, and *Charity* favored by the
Puritans.

—— I ——

### Ingrid

Scandinavian, "hero's child." Var: **Inga, Inge, Inger.**
The name of an ancient Norse god of fertility and
prosperity, Ing became the basis for a number of related
Scandinavian names all having to do with heroes and
heroic deeds. This one is probably the best known because of Ingrid Bergman, star of *Casablanca* and other
movie classics.

### Irene

Greek, "peace." Var: **Eirene, Irena, Irina, Rena,
Rene, Renie, Rina.**
The goddess of peace in Greek mythology, Irene was
called Pax by the Romans. Popular in Europe around the
eighteenth century and still later in England, the name

only became fashionable in the United States early in the 1900s. It can be pronounced as either two or three syllables; two is common in American usage.

## Iris

Greek, "rainbow." Var: **Irisa.**

The Greeks saw the rainbow as a bridge from the gods to humans, and so Iris, goddess of the rainbow, also served as a messenger. The range of colors found in the rainbow accounts for the name of the iris flower and the colored portion of the eye. Novelist Iris Murdoch.

## Isabel

Hebrew, "God's oath." Var: **Bella, Belle, Isa, Isabele, Isabella, Isabelle, Isobel, Issie.**

See **Elizabeth.** In the Middle Ages, this variation of the biblical name spread from French royalty to Spain and Scotland. The Spanish queen Isabella sponsored the voyage of discovery by Columbus in 1492.

## Ivy

Old English, "ivy plant." Var: **Ivey.**

Another flower and plant name that came into use at the end of the nineteenth century. A symbol of faithfulness. *For Love of Ivy* was a popular film of the 1960s.

— **J** —

## Jacqueline

Hebrew, "following after, supplanting." Var: **Jacki, Jackie, Jaclyn, Jacquelyn, Jacquetta, Jacqui.**

A feminine version of the French *Jacques* (see **Jacob**

and **James**). As with many other French names, it was
widely favored in England during the later Middle Ages,
but it began to decline in popularity in the Elizabethan
era. It was revived less than one hundred years ago and
took on new life in the 1960s when John F. Kennedy and
his wife, Jacqueline, were in the White House. Novelist
Jackie Collins.

## Jamie

Hebrew, "following after, supplanting." Var: **Jaime,
Jaimie, Jayme.**

A Scottish form of *James* that has recently been adopted
as a girl's name in the United States. The Spanish variant
*Jaime* is properly pronounced "high-may." Actress Jamie
Lee Curtis.

## Jane

Hebrew, "God is gracious." Var: **Jan, Jana, Janella,
Janelle, Janet, Janetta, Janette, Janey, Jani, Janice,
Janie, Janina, Janine, Janis, Jayne, Jen, Jenny.** See
also **Jean, Joan, Joanne.**

In its long history, this feminine version of *John* shows
how the popularity of many different forms of one name
can rise and fall over the centuries.

It evolved originally from the Hebrew *Johanna*, which
appears as *Joanna* in the New Testament. In the Middle
Ages, *Joan* was the version adopted in England, and it
remained fashionable for about three hundred years. The
proof that it preceded other variations is demonstrated by
the fact that the French heroine Jeanne d'Arc of the early
1400s was known in England as Joan of Arc.

In the sixteenth century, *Jane*, from the Old French
*Jehane*, made its appearance, and it, too, held favor for
about three centuries. One of the first historical figures
to have the name was Jane Seymour, Henry VIII's third

wife. After the Protestant Reformation, the Puritans made *Joanna* its chief rival; toward the end of its popularity, *Jane* managed to survive in a combined form (*Mary Jane*). In the nineteenth century, *Jean*, another form of *Jehane*, came into fashion in the United States and England, arriving not directly from France but via Scotland, where it had already established itself.

There was a revival of both *Joan* and *Jane* earlier in the present century, but now the wheel has turned again, and *Joanne* and even the original *Johanna* are making a return. Actress Jane Fonda; TV anchorwoman Jane Pauley; singer Janis Joplin.

## Jasmin

Persian, "jasmine plant." Var: **Jasmina, Jasmine, Jess, Jessamine, Jessamy, Jessamyn, Jessie.**

As *Yasmin*, this is a familiar name for girls in Arab countries. It was introduced with other flower names in England around the turn of the century, but its principal interest now lies in its sharing some shorter forms with the popular *Jessica*.

## Jean

Hebrew, "God is gracious." Var: **Jeanette, Jeanie, Jeanne, Jeannette, Jeannie, Jeannine.**

See **Jane.** Popular in Scotland for more than a century before it was taken up in America and England in the 1800s. One of the most famous celebrations of the name is the lyric addressed to his wife by the Scottish poet Robert Burns. Actress Jean Simmons.

## Jennifer

Welsh, "white spirit." Var: **Jen, Jenifer, Jennie, Jenny.**

A form given in Cornwall to *Guinevere*, the name of King Arthur's queen. The original name has long since passed out of fashion, but *Jennifer*, limited for centuries mainly to a small corner of England, has become since the 1950s one of the most popular names for girls in that country. It is even more popular in this country, where it has appeared consistently in most lists of the top ten since the early 1970s, usually in first place. Its sudden American rise is credited to the success of Erich Segal's *Love Story*, in which it is the name of the heroine.

## Jessica

Hebrew, "God sees." Var: **Jess, Jesse, Jessi, Jessie, Jessy.** See also **Jasmin.**

Like *Jennifer*, but even more recently, this relatively uncommon name has had a dramatic rise in popularity. In one form it appears early in the Old Testament, but it may also be a feminine version of *Jesse*, the name of King David's father, and in that case the probable meaning is "wealthy." Its best known literary use is in Shakespeare's *The Merchant of Venice*. Actress Jessica Lange.

## Joan

Hebrew, "God is gracious." Var: **Joanie, Joni, Jonie, Jonna.**

See **Jane.** The feminine version of *John* that was in common use during the Middle Ages, *Joan* practically disappeared after that until its return in the 1920s. Now it is in decline again. Singers Joni Mitchell, Joan Baez.

## Joanne

Hebrew, "God is gracious." Var: **Jo, Joana, Joann, Joanna, Johanna.**

This early form of *Jane* appears in the Gospel of Luke as *Joanna*, the name of one of the "ministering women" who followed Jesus and the disciples. It was revived as an alternative to *Jane* in the seventeenth century and has made regular reappearances since then. *Joanne* is currently the most popular version, but *Johanna* seems to be on the rise. Previously it was also written as *Jo-Anne*, indicating a combined name, but this is seldom seen today. Actress Joanne Woodward.

## Jocelyn

Old German, "from the Goths." Var: **Jocelin, Joscelyn, Josselyn, Joycelin.**
See **Joyce.** A variation introduced among the Germans early in the Middle Ages, it faded from use by the fifteenth century. It was in fashion briefly about fifty years ago, especially in England, and is again attracting some attention.

## Jodie

Hebrew, "object of praise." Var: **Jodi, Jody.** See also the masculine **Jody** and **Joseph.**
This modern short form of *Judith* appears to have caught up with *Judy*, its predecessor. In the past it was used mainly for boys. Actress Jodie Foster.

## Joelle

Hebrew, "Jehovah is God." Var: **Joela, Joella, Joellen.**
There is a Book of Joel in the Old Testament, and the masculine form is also found in many other biblical texts. Like the masculine *Joel*, the feminine form has recently been revived along with other Old Testament names.

# Joy

Latin, "joy, happiness." Var: **Joya, Joye.**

It is often listed as a short form of *Joyce*, but there is no original connection between the two. The apparent similarity probably arises not only from the spelling but because both were revived at about the same time in the late nineteenth century.

# Joyce

Old French, "from the Goths." Var: **Joice, Joyse.** See also **Jocelyn, Joy.**

Its introduction into English was derived from *Joisse*, the French version of a saint's name in seventh-century Brittany. It became a family name in Ireland and was used during the Middle Ages as a first name for both boys and girls. When it returned about one hundred years ago, this dual use persisted for a time: American poet Joyce Kilmer was a soldier in World War I. Now the name is feminine.

# Judith

Hebrew, "object of praise." Var: **Judi, Judie, Judy, Judye.** See also **Jodie.**

Originally it meant simply "from Judah," or a Jewish woman. It is recorded in the Book of Genesis as the name of Esau's first wife; it is also one of the books of the Apocrypha, those not accepted by the Hebrew and Protestant faiths. In the latter story, often adapted by poets and dramatists, Judith is a beautiful heroine who attracts and then slays Holofernes, commander of the invading Assyrian army. The name appeared in England sometime in the ninth century, but it was not until the end of the seventeenth century, with the introduction of the first Punch and Judy puppet shows, that this variation gained wide popularity. Hollywood star Judy Garland; TV news-woman Judy Woodruff.

## Julia

Latin, "downy hair." Var: **Juli, Julie, Juliet, Julietta, Juliette**. See also **Juliana**.

The feminine form of the name of a distinguished Roman *gens* or clan, whose most celebrated member was Julius Caesar. Relatives who had the name included his aunt, sister, and daughter. Because of Caesar's fame, it was popular as a first name in the Roman empire, then gave way to a number of variations.

It was taken up as a literary name by Shakespeare, who borrowed *Juliet* from the Italian *Giulietta*, and especially by Robert Herrick, whose series of poems to Julia made the name fashionable in the seventeenth century. Cooking expert Julia Child; actress Julie Andrews.

## Juliana

Latin, "downy hair." Var: **Juliane, Juliann, Julianna, Julianne, Julina, Juline, Leane, Leanne, Liana**. See also **Gillian**.

A variant of *Julia* that emerged during the Middle Ages as a feminine form of *Julian*, which had been used until then for both girls and boys. It became well established in the Netherlands as a name for daughters in the royal family. Other forms have generally been more popular in the United States.

## June

Latin, "month of June." Var: **Junette, Junia, Junie**.

In Roman mythology, Juno was the queen of heaven, a goddess of women and childbirth, the wife of Jupiter and mother of Mars. The masculine *Junius* was also the name of a patrician Roman clan. Like other first names taken from months, it was introduced less than a century ago.

## — K —

### Karen

Greek, "pure." Var: **Caren, Carin, Caryn, Karin, Karyn.**

See **Katharine.** The Danish version of the name, adopted first in the United States and then in other English-speaking countries. It was especially popular in the 1950s. Actress Karen Valentine.

### Katharine

Greek, "pure." Var: **Katalin, Kate, Katerina, Katerine, Katey, Kath, Kathe, Katherine, Kathi, Kathie, Kathleen, Kathryn, Kathy, Katie, Katrina, Katya, Kay, Kettie, Kit, Kittie, Kitty.** See also **Catherine, Karen.**

This very old name is still a favorite and offers a variety of forms to choose from, many of which have taken on an identity of their own. *Katharine* is probably closest to the original form. Its beginnings have not been firmly established, but it seems to have spread with the veneration of Katharine of Alexandria, a martyr of the fourth century. According to legend, she refused to renounce her Christian faith despite the command of the ruler of Egypt. She was tortured on a spiked wheel, which was later named for her and became her symbol; today it's the name of a spinning fireworks display. Her shrine is in a monastery on Mount Sinai.

The name and the legend apparently spread to Europe in the twelfth century as a result of the Crusades. At first it was *Catherine* in France and *Katharine* in England, but the two spellings and their variations soon became more a matter of fashion than of language. It was a favorite name among royalty in many countries; three of Henry VIII's queens and two empresses of Russia had the name, one of them Catherine the Great. It is also the name of the patron of Italy.

In England, *Kate* seems to have been the first of the popular short forms. It is the pet name of the heroine in Shakespeare's *The Taming of the Shrew*. Early in the eighteenth century it was largely replaced by *Kitty*, a popular name for actresses of that period. Still later came *Kathy* and more recently *Kay*.

## Kelly

Irish, "warrior." Var: **Kellee, Kelley, Kelli.**
An Irish family name that sprang into popularity as a feminine first name in the 1960s. Some researchers suggest that the similar *Keely* is a variant, but others trace it to another Irish surname meaning "graceful."

## Kerry

Irish, "dark." Var: **Keri, Kerri, Kerrie.**
It is also an Irish place name. Originally used for boys, it became fashionable for girls about the same time as *Kelly*, but without the same impact.

## Kimberly

Old English, "royal fortress meadow." Var: **Kim, Kimberley, Kimbra.** See also the masculine **Kimball.**
This name began its ascension as a feminine form

about thirty years ago, when actresses Kim Novak, Kim Stanley, and Kim Hunter were appearing regularly in movies. It has declined slightly but is still popular.

## Kristin

Latin, "follower of Christ." Var: **Kirsten, Kirstin, Kristen, Kristi, Kristie, Kristina, Kristine, Kristy.**

See **Christina.** For the most part these are Scandinavian forms, but *Kirsten* and others are also found in Scotland. They began to appear in the United States in the 1950s. Actress Kristy McNichol.

— L —

## Laura

Latin, "laurel or bay tree." Var: **Lara, Laure, Laurel, Lauretta, Laurette, Laurey, Lauri, Laurie, Laurinda, Lora, Loretta, Lorette, Lorinda, Lorita.** See also **Lauren, Lorraine.**

It probably developed as a short form of *Laurencia,* the feminine of *Laurence* (or *Lawrence,* as preferred in the United States). It was already established by the thirteenth century, but early in the following century it gained enduring fame because of the series of sonnets written to the lady of that name by the Italian poet Petrarch. As with Dante's Beatrice, he made her a symbol of ideal love that was adopted by poets of many succeeding centuries. Different variations have come and gone over the years, and yet *Laura* itself has retained its popularity. A 1940s film of that name has become a classic, along with its theme music. The Russian *Lara* is the name of one of the leading characters in the novel and film *Doctor Zhivago.*

From ancient times, the laurel wreath has meant the bestowing of high honors, as in the title of poet laureate. *Laura* may have survived partly because of this long tradition. It's interesting to note that the Greek name derived from the same tree, *Daphne*, became fashionable only at the end of the nineteenth century and is seldom used now. Children's author Laura Ingalls Wilder.

## Lauren

Latin, "laurel or bay tree." Var: **Laureen, Laurina, Loreen, Loren, Lorena, Lorene, Lurena, Lurene.**

A variant of *Laura* made popular by two fashion models who became actresses, Lauren Bacall and Lauren Hutton. *Loren*, *Lorne*, and similar forms are also masculine names from *Lawrence*.

## Leigh

Old English, "meadow." Var: **Lea, Lee.**

It has been suggested that this name is derived from the Old Testament *Leah*, but the same element appears in many names based on Old English words (see below). The Hebrew root of *Leah* is variously given as "weary," "wild cow," and "mistress."

## Lesley

Old English, "small meadow." Var: **Les, Leslie.**

Taken from a Scottish place name and family name. With few exceptions, it has been given as a feminine name only in this century. The *-ley* spelling has generally been used for girls in the past, but the two seem to be interchangeable now. TV newswoman Leslie Stahl; actress Lesley Ann Warren.

## Lillian

Latin, "lily plant." Var: **Lil, Lila, Lili, Lilia, Lilian, Lilli, Lillie, Lilly, Lily.**

In its original form this name dates back to the Elizabethan era, and it may have been used then as a short form of *Elizabeth* (*Lilibeth*). As the more modern *Lily*, it came into use with other flower names in the late nineteenth century. "Miss Lillian" Carter, mother of the thirty-ninth United States president.

## Linda

Spanish, "pretty." Var: **Lin, Lindy, Lyn, Lynda, Lynn, Lynne.**

There are several possible derivations for this popular name. The oldest is a short form of names like *Ethelinda* dating from the Middle Ages; the *-lind* element comes from an Old German word meaning "serpent," a symbol of wisdom. Another possibility is a short form of the names created by poets and playwrights of the Restoration period (see **Belinda**). The problem with these suggestions is that *Linda* was not widely used in English until the late nineteenth century, when a variety of new names were introduced. This makes the Spanish origin seem the most logical. Actress Linda Evans; singer Linda Ronstadt.

## Lindsay

Old English, "linden island." Var: **Lin, Lindsey, Lyn, Lyndsay, Lyndsey, Lynsay, Lynsey.**

Another English name taken from a family name and a place name in Scotland. It became fashionable as a girl's name in the United States only in the last fifty years. Actress Lindsay Wagner.

## Liza

Hebrew, "God's oath." Var: **Lisa, Lise, Lisette, Lissie, Liz, Lizzie, Lizzy.**

See **Elizabeth.** In one form or another, this short version has had a separate identity for nearly a century. In the early 1900s it was the nickname ("tin lizzie") for the most popular American car ever built, the Ford Model T. Columnist Liz Smith; actress Liza Minnelli.

## Lorna

Old English, "forsaken." Var: **Lorne.** See also the masculine **Lawrence.**

Although some authors suggest that this was originally derived from *Laura*, based on the association with the masculine form, it seems more likely that the name was the creation of the nineteenth-century novelist Richard D. Blackmore, whose romantic adventure *Lorna Doone* was highly successful.

## Lorraine

French, "from Lorraine." Var: **Laraine, Larayne, Loraine, Lorayne, Lori, Lorie, Lory, Lorrayne, Lorri, Lorrie, Lorry.**

Many of these forms are usually associated with *Laura*, but the name may also come from Alsace-Lorraine, a French region bordering on West Germany. Joan of Arc was known as Joan of Lorraine. The name was popular in the United States in the period between the two World Wars. Playwright Lorraine Hansberry.

## Louise

Old German, "famous warrior." Var: **Aloise, Aloyse, Eloise, Heloise, Lois, Loise, Lou, Louisa, Lu, Luisa, Luise, Lulu.**

The feminine of *Louis*. It was very popular in France beginning in the Middle Ages, but it was not introduced in England until the seventeenth century. The name was particularly fashionable in the United States in the nineteenth century, when Louisa May Alcott wrote her *Little Women*. *Eloise* was found often in the 1950s, but neither masculine nor feminine forms are widely used today.

## Lucy

Latin, "light." Var: **Luce, Lucia, Luciana, Lucie, Lucile, Lucilla, Lucille, Lucina, Lucinda.**

There was a Roman *gens* or clan named *Lucius*, and Lucina was, with Juno, a goddess of childbirth. However, the popularity of the name comes originally from a Christian martyr of the fourth century, Lucia of Sicily. It has been used since the Middle Ages, and it was a special favorite in England in the late seventeenth century. It gained attention more recently with actress Lucille Ball's long-running TV series *I Love Lucy*.

## — M —

## Madeline

Hebrew, "from Magdala. Var: **Lena, Lina, Madalena, Maddy, Madelaine, Madeleine, Madelena, Madelina, Madelon, Madlyn, Mady, Magda, Magdalena, Magdalene.** See also **Marlene.**

According to the New Testament, the birthplace of Mary Magdalene was Magdala on the Sea of Galilee; the word may originally have meant "tower." One of the most loyal followers of Jesus, she was widely venerated in the Middle Ages, when the two names were given together. As a separate name, the French *Madeleine*, spelled in a number of ways, later became popular. Singer Lena Horne; actress Madeline Kahn.

## Marcia

Latin, "martial." Var: **Marcella, Marcelle, Marcie, Marcille, Marcy, Marsha.**

From *Marcius*, a Roman clan name probably derived from Mars, the god of war. It was fashionable in the nineteenth century along with the masculine *Mark* and again in the mid-twentieth century. Now the masculine form is making a strong return, but *Marcia* is moving at a slower pace. Pulitzer Prize-winning playwright (1983) Marsha Norman; author Marcia Davenport.

## Margaret

Persian, "child of light." Var: **Greta, Gretchen, Grete, Gretta, Madge, Maggie, Maggy, Maisie, Marga, Margareta, Margaretha, Margaretta, Margarette, Margarita, Margaux, Marge, Margery, Margherita, Margie, Margit, Margo, Margot, Margret, Marguerite, Margy, Marji, Marjorie, Meta, Peg, Pegeen, Peggy, Rita.** See also **Megan.**

As the list of variations indicates, this old name appears in many different languages, and for that reason there is disagreement about its origin. The daisy is also called marguerite, from the French word, and a similar word in Greek means "pearl." But the root probably goes back even further, since the first *Margaret* we know about was an early (and possibly legendary) martyr in Syria.

It was the name of a Scottish queen in the eleventh century, and from that time on it has been a royal name in nearly every country in Europe. The younger sister of today's Queen Elizabeth is Princess Margaret. Because it is also the name of several saints, it lost favor during the Protestant Reformation of the 1500s, but by the mid-nineteenth century it was again frequently found. The two most popular short forms in the United States fifty years ago, *Peggy* and *Rita*, are seldom given today.

English prime minister Margaret Thatcher; actress-model Margaux Hemingway; marathon runner Grete Waitz.

## Marianne

Hebrew, "bitterness." Var: **Marian, Mariana, Marianna, Marion, Maryann, Maryanne.** See also **Anne.**

See **Mary.** The practice of combining names was prevalent in the eighteenth century, and *Mary* and *Anne* were the two most often used together. This served to conceal the fact that the name has also had its own identity as a form of *Mary* since medieval times. It originated in France as *Marion*, which was used for both girls and boys. The feminine version later became *Marian*, a name associated in England with the Robin Hood legend (Maid Marian). Still later it was extended to *Marianne*, who personifies the French republic in the same way that Uncle Sam represents the United States. Singer Marian Anderson.

## Marlene

Hebrew, "Mary, from Magdala." Var: **Marilin, Marilyn, Marleen, Marlena, Marline.**

See **Madeline**, which was one result of the shortening of Mary Magdalene. Another was the contraction of the two names into *Marlene* and related forms, perhaps in eighteenth-century Germany. Two famous actresses: Marlene Dietrich, Marilyn Monroe.

## Martha

Aramaic, "lady." Var: **Marta, Marthe, Marti, Martita.**

A language related to Hebrew, Aramaic was spoken in the Middle East for about five hundred years before and after the time of Christ. In the New Testament, Martha is the sister of Mary Magdalene and of Lazarus; Jesus was a guest in her house in Bethany. During the medieval period the name was popular in France as *Marthe*, but it wasn't adopted in England until after the Protestant Reformation, when it was linked by the Puritans to the idea of hospitality. Martha Custis Washington was the wife of the first United States president.

## Mary

Hebrew, "bitterness." Var: **Mame, Mamie, Mara, Maria, Marie, Mariel, Marietta, Mariette, Marita, Marya, Mia, Mimi, Min, Minna, Minnie.** See also **Marianne, Marlene, Maureen, May, Miriam, Molly.**

Veneration of the mother of Jesus began about the sixth century, and though it was set back by the Protestant Reformation, it continued to spread in largely Catholic nations. For several hundred years the name was considered too sacred to be used directly, and in some countries substitutes were adopted (see **Carmen, Dolores**). However, when it came into general use, about the twelfth century, first as *Marie* in France, it gradually grew in popularity to the point that other forms evolved naturally.

This variety has made it difficult to detect the original meaning, and some researchers estimate that more than fifty different explanations have been put forward. For example, one common belief is that it is associated with the sea because of the Latin *mare*, and Mary is viewed as the patron of sailors and sea voyagers. Another possibility derives from its first appearance in the Old Testament as *Miriam*, defined as "longed-for child." But the definition generally accepted is from the Hebrew *marrah*, or "bitterness."

By the Victorian period, *Mary* in one form or another was probably the favorite name in the United States, England, and Ireland, as well as in France, and though it has declined in the past thirty years, it is still very popular. Mary Todd Lincoln, wife of the sixteenth United States president; Mamie Doud Eisenhower, wife of the thirty-fourth president; opera star Maria Callas; actress Mia Farrow.

## Maureen

Irish, "little Mary." Var: **Maura, Maure, Maurene, Maurine, Moira, Moyra.**

Until recently this form of *Maure*, the Irish for *Mary*, was a favorite with American families, but in some areas it seems to be losing ground to *Moira*, one of the group of Irish names currently in fashion. Actress-dancer Moira Shearer, star of the film classic *The Red Shoes* (1948).

## May

Latin, "great." Var: **Mae, Maia, Maya, Maye.**

A month name from the Roman earth goddess Maia. In Greek mythology, she was one of the seven daughters of Atlas, who were changed into the star constellation known as the Pleiades. The name was frequently seen in the nineteenth century but generally as a form of *Mary*. Actress Mae West.

## Megan

Welsh, "little Margaret." Var: **Meaghan, Meg, Meggie, Meggy, Meghan.**

See **Margaret.** This is a Celtic name found in both Wales and Ireland; it has gained a strong foothold in the United States since the early 1970s. It may be that *Peggy*, a pet form of *Margaret*, evolved as a children's rhyme with *Meggy*. Playwright Megan Terry.

## Melanie

Greek, "dark." Var: **Melania, Melany, Mellie, Milena.**

A name introduced from France to England in the seventeenth century. It has only recently become popular there and in the United States, even though it first reached a wide audience nearly fifty years ago because of a character in Margaret Mitchell's *Gone With the Wind*.

## Melinda

Old English, "mild." Var: **Amelinda, Linda, Malinda, Malinde, Melindy.**

This can be traced back even further than its Old English root to Greek and Latin words meaning "soft, gentle." Even so, it was probably a literary creation of the late seventeenth century, along with *Amanda* and similar names. Its popularity has grown in the past decade.

## Melissa

Greek, "bee." Var: **Lissa, Lisse, Melessa, Melisa, Melise, Melisse, Millie, Milly, Missie, Missy.**

Like *Melinda*, it came into use about three hundred years ago and is currently being revived, but with even greater success. In one version of a Greek legend, Melissa was a nymph who fed goat's milk to the infant Zeus, later the supreme god. Because she knew the secret of collecting honey, she was changed into a bee. Singer Melissa Manchester.

## Merle

French, "blackbird." Var: **Merl, Merlina, Merline, Merrill, Meryl, Myrl.**

Used in the past for both girls and boys, this bird's name was adopted in English in the nineteenth century. Today it is primarily a girl's name. Two famous actresses: Merle Oberon of the 1930s and 1940s, and Academy Award-winner (1982) Meryl Streep.

## Michelle

Hebrew, "who is like God?" Var: **Michaela, Michele, Micheline, Micki, Mickie, Micky, Miguela, Miguelita.**

Both the masculine and feminine versions of this name have been on top-ten lists since the late 1960s. However, the masculine form was first used about the twelfth century, while *Michelle*, one of several French forms, was seldom given in English until the World War II period. Its sudden popularity may have been helped by the Beatles' song of the same name.

## Mildred

Old English, "gentle power." Var: **Mildrid, Milli, Millie, Milly.**

The Anglo-Saxons found it difficult to resist adding a note of force to a name, even when the other half of the name, as in *Mildred*, conveyed the idea of gentleness. It was brought to attention in medieval England by a seventh-century St. Mildred. Like many similiar names, it was revived by the Victorians; its high point in this country came early in the 1900s. Actress Joan Crawford won an Academy Award for her role in *Mildred Pierce* (1945).

## Millicent

Old German, "work strength." Var: **Melisande, Melesina, Melesine, Milicent, Milli, Millie, Millisent, Milly.**

Though German in origin, this name spread from France in the Middle Ages based on a French fairy tale. There are several different versions, but the common thread is that the heroine must conceal from her beloved the secret that at certain times she changes from her human shape into another form. It was adapted into an opera in 1902, *Pelleas and Melisande*, with music by Claude Debussy.

## Miranda

Latin, "admirable." Var: **Mandy, Mira.**

Probably invented by Shakespeare. It is the name of the magician Prospero's lovely daughter in *The Tempest*. It has been given regularly but not very widely since the Elizabethan period.

## Miriam

Hebrew, "longed-for child." Var: **Minnie, Miryam, Mitzi.**

Mentioned for the first time in the Book of Exodus, it is the name of the sister of Moses and Aaron. Most authorities agree that it is the earliest written form of *Mary*, and the same Hebrew root is sometimes given for both names, but there is no definitely established meaning for either one. It was adopted by the Puritans in the seventeenth century.

## Molly

Irish, "Mary." Var: **Moll, Mollie.** See also **Polly.**

This has long been a familiar form of *Mary*. In the

late eighteenth century it almost passed out of use when "moll" was established as a slang term for the female companion of a criminal, due in part to Daniel Defoe's *Moll Flanders*, the story of a girl pickpocket. But this definition has become old-fashioned by now, and *Molly* has returned to favor.

## Muriel

Irish, "sea bright." Var: **Murial, Murielle.**

Sometimes given as an Irish form of *Mary* or as a variation of *Meryl*, this name can also be traced to an Irish word linked to the sea. Novelist Muriel Spark; poet Muriel Rukeyser.

# — N —

## Nadine

Russian, "hope." Var: **Nadia, Nadie, Nadina, Nadya.** See also **Hope.**

The latest in a series of Russian names—this is actually a French variation—that were introduced in England and the United States toward the end of the nineteenth century. Others, seldom seen now, are *Olga* and *Sonia*. Olympic gymnast Nadia Comaneci; author Nadine Gordimer.

## Nancy

Hebrew, "grace." Var: **Nan, Nana, Nance, Nancee, Nanci, Nancie, Nanette, Nanine, Nanon, Nannie, Nanny.**

See **Anne.** The first major variations were *Nan*, which

appears in Shakespeare's plays, and *Nanny*, a familiar term for a children's nurse. *Nancy* came later, during a revival of *Anne* in the eighteenth century under Queen Anne of Britain. It was one of the earliest pet names to stand on its own. Nancy Drew was the heroine of a series of popular mystery novels begun in the 1930s for young girls. (Anne) Nancy Davis Reagan, wife of the fortieth president.

## Naomi

Hebrew, "pleasant." Var: **Naoma, Noemi, Nomi.**

Ruth's mother-in-law in the Book of Ruth. It was another of the biblical names taken up by the Puritans after the Reformation. It seems to have been forgotten in the current revival of Old Testament names, but its chance may still be coming.

## Natalie

Latin, "birthday." Var: **Natala, Natalia, Natasha, Natasia, Natassia, Nathalia, Nathalie.**

Although the original meaning refers to a birthday generally, its regular use in a Latin phrase for the birth of Jesus (*natale domini*) has made it a synonym for Christmas, as with the French *Noel* and feminine *Noelle*. It has long been a favorite in Russia, and a variant, *Natasha*, is the name of the heroine in Tolstoy's *War and Peace*. Hollywood star Natalie Wood.

## Nicole

Greek, "victory of the people." Var: **Nicki, Nicky, Nicola, Nicoletta, Nicolette, Niki, Nikki.** See also **Colette.**

Feminine versions of this name have been popular since the Middle Ages. For a long time the Italian *Nicola* was preferred in England, but it has since been overtaken by the French *Nicole*, which is now very much in fashion in the United States. It is the name of the heroine in F. Scott Fitzgerald's last completed novel, *Tender Is the Night*, also a movie.

## Nina

Spanish, "little girl." Var: **Ninetta, Ninette, Ninon.**

In English this is generally taken as a variation of *Anne*, possibly from a French form, *Nanine*. It can also be traced to a Russian form of *Anne*. But it seems even more likely that it shows the influence of the Spanish word defined above, the name of one of the three ships in the first voyage of Christopher Columbus. Singer Nina Simone; designer Nina Ricci.

## Norma

Latin, "rule, measurement." Var: **Nora, Normie.**

An alternative definition may be as the feminine of *Norman*. Its principal claim to attention is an early nineteenth-century Bellini opera of the same name. It was fashionable in the first decade of this century but is not often given now. The title character in *Norma Rae*, for which Sally Field won an Academy Award in 1979.

## — O —

## Odetta

Old German, "fatherland." Var: **Odele, Odelia, Odella, Odelle, Odette, Odile, Othelia, Ottilie, Uta.**

Like many Old German names, it goes back to the twelfth century in England; sometimes it is traced to the feminine of *Otto*, which would make the meaning "prosperous." As the French forms *Odette* and, less frequently, *Odile*, it has had slight periods of popularity, but *Odetta* is better known today, perhaps because of the singer of that name.

## Olivia

Greek, "olive tree." Var: **Liva, Livvie, Livvy, Livy, Oliva, Olive, Olivetta, Olivette.**

This name is often regarded as the feminine of *Oliver*, but most researchers agree that it has a different origin and that it is directly related to the tree and its fruit. As a source of food, fuel, and soap, the tree has been important since ancient times. The offering of an olive branch was (and figuratively still is) a symbol of peace; the olive wreath also preceded the laurel as a recognition of success. In its first English form, *Oliva*, it was in use about the thirteenth century, but three centuries later Shakespeare's *Twelfth Night* brought *Olivia* to attention, and this form has always been better known in the United States. Singer Olivia Newton-John; actress Olivia de Havilland.

## — P —

## Pamela

Greek, "all honey." Var: **Pam, Pamella, Pammie, Pammy.**

It was created in the sixteenth century by Sir Philip Sidney, the same poet responsible for *Stella* (see **Estelle**). But as with that name, it took a subsequent author, Samuel Richardson, to bring it into fashion. Written as a series of letters, his *Pamela* (1740) is one of the earliest novels in English literature. The name achieved its greatest success in the United States in the middle of this century. Tennis star Pam Shriver.

## Patricia

Latin, "of nobility." Var: **Pat, Patrice, Patrizia, Patsy, Patti, Patty, Tricia, Trish, Trisha.**

Unlike the masculine form, *Patrick*, which became well known because of the fifth-century patron saint of Ireland, *Patricia* was not adopted until much later, sometime in the eighteenth century, and then it was introduced from Scotland and not from Ireland. It became gradually popular in the early 1900s, when *Patsy* was a familiar short form, but its popularity faded as this version took on the slang meaning of a gullible person. In other forms the name was recently revived. Singer Patti Smith; actress Patty Duke.

## Paula

Latin, "small." Var: **Paola, Paolina, Paule, Paulena, Paulene, Pauletta, Paulette, Paulina, Pauline.** See also **Polly.**

The name of a fourth-century Roman saint, the feminine version of *Paul* has been used since the Middle Ages, but it was not often found until the present century, when there was a renewal of interest in both forms. *Paulette* and *Pauline* were fashionable in nineteenth-century France; the latter was the name of a sister of Napoleon. Actress Paula Prentiss.

## Pearl

Latin, "sea stone." Var: **Pearla, Pearle, Perla, Perle.** Like most other jewel names, it was introduced at the end of the nineteenth century, which accounts for its frequency in the early years of this century: author Pearl Buck; silent-movie actress Pearl White. The jewel names are not often given today. Singer Pearl Bailey.

## Penelope

Greek, "weaver." Var: **Pen, Pennie, Penny.**

Possibly the original Greek word meant "bobbin," or a spool for thread used in weaving, and from this it acquired the meaning of the person engaged in that work. The same kind of activity is linked to the most famous classical bearer of the name, the wife of Ulysses in Homer's *Odyssey*. When her husband was assumed to be dead during his absence of ten years, Penelope agreed to marry again after the tapestry she was weaving had been completed. She put off her suitors by undoing each day's work the same evening. The name came into use in England in the seventeenth century. Today it is generally found in a shorter form. Actress Penny Marshall.

## Petula

Latin, "seeker." Var: **Pet, Petulia.**

Although it may possibly be a variation of a feminine form of *Peter*, this unusual name seems to have only two recent associations: a popular film of the 1960s (*Petulia*) and English singer Petula Clark.

## Phyllis

Greek, "green branch." Var: **Philis, Phillis, Phyl, Phylisse.** See also **Felicia.**

According to Greek legend, Phyllis was a maiden who died for love (the reasons vary) and was changed into an almond tree. A name popular among Greek and Roman poets, it was revived by seventeenth-century pastoral poets in England and Scotland; as a result of overuse, it became so closely identified with the image of a country maiden tending her flock that it practically vanished by the late 1700s. It was introduced again one hundred years ago, becoming fashionable for a brief period early in this century. Poet Phyllis McGinley.

## Polly

Latin, "small." Var: **Poll, Pollie.** See also **Paula.**
This is a definition of the name as a form of *Paula*, which it often is, but it may also have developed as a rhyme with *Molly*, in the same way as *Peggy* is said to have evolved from *Meggy* (see **Megan**). Eleanor Porter's *Pollyanna*, a novel from the early 1900s whose young heroine helped everyone to see the bright side of life, was a successful 1960s film. Actress Polly Bergen.

## Priscilla

Latin, "of ancient time." Var: **Pris, Priscella, Priss, Pross.**
A New Testament name that found great favor with the Puritans in the seventeenth century, it was very popular in early American settlements (as in Longfellow's "The Courtship of Miles Standish"). The name was revived in the late 1800s in England and the United States, but it is not often found today. Actress Priscilla Beaulieu Presley.

## Prudence

Latin, "provident, careful." Var: **Pru, Prudi, Prudy, Prue.**
Another of the Puritans' abstract virtue names, but it first appeared at least two hundred years before the Prot-

estant Reformation. Unlike many of the longer names of this type, it never dropped out of use, although it is rare at present.

# — Q —

## Queena

Old English, "queen." Var: **Queenie, Queeny.**

A name dating from the Middle Ages, it had a slight degree of popularity in England during the long reign of Queen Victoria in the nineteenth century. Occasionally, it was also a nickname for *Regina*, from the Latin word for queen (she was called Victoria Regina).

## Quentin

Latin, "fifth." Var: **Quintin, Quintina.** See also the masculine **Quentin.**

Primarily a boy's name from Scotland, it has sometimes been adopted as a name for girls. This may have received some support from its use by author and Nobel laureate William Faulkner in his novel, later a movie, *The Sound and the Fury*. *Queta* and *Quita* are names sometimes seen today that may be derived from the same Latin root.

# — R —

## Rachel

Hebrew, "ewe." Var: **Rae, Rachele, Rachelle, Raquel, Raquela.** See also **Rochelle**, **Shelley.**

In the Book of Genesis, Rachel was the sister of Leah and the rival with her for marriage with Jacob; he loved Rachel but was tricked into marrying Leah first. The name has been consistently popular in Jewish communities, but it wasn't used more widely until it was taken up by the Puritans in the seventeenth century. Since then it has regularly had periods of fashion and is enjoying one now. Actresses Rachel Roberts, Raquel Welch.

## Rebecca

Hebrew, "bound, tied." Var: **Becki, Becky, Reba, Rebeca, Rebeka, Rebekah, Reeba, Riva, Rivkah, Rivy.**

Another current favorite, with a history similar to that of *Rachel*. The first Rebecca, in Genesis, was the wife of Isaac and the mother of Esau and Jacob. It is the name of two famous characters in literature: Becky Sharp in William Thackeray's *Vanity Fair*, and the mysterious first wife in *Rebecca*, by Daphne du Maurier, made into a film classic by Alfred Hitchcock.

## Regan

Latin, "queen." Var: **Reagan, Reghan.**

This Celtic variation of *Regina* was given by Shakespeare to one of the three daughters in *King Lear*. Seldom found in England, it has recently been gaining in popularity in this country.

## Robin

Old German, "bright fame." Var: **Robbi, Robbie, Robby, Robina, Robinia, Robyn.** See also the masculine **Robert.**

A name with a twofold history: as a short form of *Roberta*, which was fashionable in the early 1900s but is rarely seen today, and as a name with its own identity since the Middle Ages, derived from the Robin Hood legend. Despite his image as a masculine hero, the name has increasingly been used for girls. Professional jockey Robyn Smith.

## Rochelle

French, "little rock." Var: **Rochella, Roshella, Roshelle.**

Sometimes regarded as a form of *Rachel*, which is found more frequently, it also has a separate origin in a French word. Playwright Rochelle Owens.

## Rosalind

Spanish, "pretty rose." Var: **Ros, Rosalinda, Rosaline, Rosalyn, Rosalynd, Roslyn, Roz, Rozalin.** See also **Rose.**

As with other names containing the *-lind* element, there are a number of possible derivations (see **Linda**). The simplest, however, and certainly the one most commonly accepted in modern times, is traced to the combination of two Spanish words, *rosa* and *linda*. It has been in regular but not wide use since the time of Shakespeare, who gave forms of it to three different characters. Long-time Hollywood star Rosalind Russell; Rosalynn Carter, wife of the thirty-ninth president.

## Rose

Latin, "rose bush." Var: **Rosa, Rosaleen, Rosalie, Rosanne, Rosanna, Rosella, Roselle, Rosetta, Rosette, Rosie, Rosina, Rosita, Rosy.** See also **Rosalind, Rosemary.**

Some researchers note that a form of this word in Old German means "horse," but it's clear that the variations of *Rose* in many different languages come from the plant and its flower, a traditional symbol of love. The Latin term derives from an earlier Greek word for the plant, seen in the name of the island of Rhodes in the Aegean Sea and in *Rhoda*, a name fashionable in the 1950s. *Rose* has been popular in England, both in its original form and a number of variations, since the twelfth century, but it seems to have reached a peak there and in the United States around 1900. As *Rosie*, it became so familiar that it designated a whole group of women factory workers during World War II (as in the song "Rosie the Riveter"). It appears in many earlier songs and poems and has a long biblical history as well. Rose Fitzgerald Kennedy, mother of the thirty-fifth president.

## Rosemary

Latin, "sea dew." Var: **Rosemarie, Rose Marie.** See also **Mary, Rose.**

Like *Marianne*, this is accepted today as a joining of two separate names, a practice common in England in the eighteenth century. But also like *Marianne*, it can stand by itself—as the Latin designation for the familiar herb, described by Ophelia in *Hamlet* as "for remembrance." It was a favorite among parents in the early 1900s. *Rosemary's Baby*, a classic thriller (by Ira Levin) and film of the 1960s. Novelist Rosemary Rogers.

## Ruth

Hebrew, "companion, friend." Var: **Ruthe, Ruthi, Ruthie, Ruthy.**

The meaning "vision of beauty" is sometimes suggested, along with "compassionate." However, the concept of a friendly companion is so closely associated with her story in the Book of Ruth that this definition is the usual one. It was adopted by the Puritans after the Reformation; some researchers speculate that this happened not so much because of its biblical reference as for its identification with an Old English word for sorrow or regret. The term survives in expressions such as "to rue the day." Actress Ruth Gordon.

# — S —

## Sally

Hebrew, "princess." Var: **Sal, Sallee, Salli, Sallie, Sallyanne.**

A variation of *Sarah* that has existed in England since the seventeenth century. It has always had a certain degree of popularity here, and possibly the fact that it is the name of America's first woman astronaut, Dr. Sally Ride, will give it a new burst of energy. Actresses Sally Field, Sally Struthers.

## Samantha

Aramaic, "listener." Var: **Sam, Sammi, Sammie.**

Along with *Martha*, this is one of the few names whose origin is traced to a language spoken in the Middle East around the time of Jesus. There all similarity ends, for while *Martha* has been a familiar name for centuries, *Samantha* has been fashionable only since the 1960s, when it was the name of the lead character in the successful TV series *Bewitched*. Although its popularity may have slipped recently, the name is still frequently given. Actress Samantha Eggar.

### Sarah

Hebrew, "princess." Var: **Sadie, Sadye, Sara, Sarena, Sarene, Sari, Sarina, Sarine, Sarita, Shari.** See also **Sally, Sharon.**

In Genesis, Sarah was the wife of Abraham and the mother of Isaac. Her name was changed from *Sarai* (which possibly means "argumentative") when her husband's was changed from *Abram*, marking the covenant established between him and the Lord.

After it was adopted at the time of the Protestant Reformation, it quickly became a favorite in England, and in the nineteenth century it was, with *Elizabeth* and *Mary*, one of the most popular names in this country as well. It was also made famous by leading actresses of the time, such as Sarah Bernhardt. It fell off slightly in the 1950s and then made a very strong comeback about ten years ago. Currently it rivals *Jessica* as the leading biblical name preference among parents of baby daughters. Unlike other traditional names, it has kept its popularity not by means of variations but through the original (or as *Sara*).

### Shana

Hebrew, "beautiful." Var: **Shaina, Shaine, Shani, Shane.** See also **Shannon.**

A number of possible origins have been proposed for this uncommon name, including a form of *Jane* and an East African word meaning "wonderful." The most appropriate explanation seems to be the one given above, but the name may also be related to the Shannon, a river in Ireland. Author and journalist Shana Alexander.

## Shannon

Irish, "wise one." Var: **Shauna, Shawna.** See also **Shana.**

Taken from the River Shannon in western Ireland and an Irish family name. It is also sometimes viewed as a feminine of *Sean* or *Shaun*. It is one of a group of Irish given and family names that became popular names for girls in the 1970s.

## Sharon

Hebrew, "plain." Var: **Shara, Shari, Sherri, Sherrie, Sherry.** See also **Sarah.**

The plain of Sharon in Israel has been noted since biblical times for its fertility and its many different flowers. The principal product today is citrus fruit. The name and its variations are occasionally linked to *Sarah,* but *Sharon* has a different origin. Because of its association with the Old Testament, it was adopted in English by the Puritans in the 1600s. It began a revival around the middle of this century.

## Sheila

Irish, "Celia." Var: **Sheela, Sheelah, Sheilah, Shelagh.**

See **Cecilia.** This Irish form has been familiar outside that country since the nineteenth century, but it became a general favorite here only in the 1940s. It was overtaken recently by a new wave of Irish names.

## Shelley

Old English, "meadow on a ridge or hilltop." Var: **Shell, Shelli, Shellie, Shelly.** See also **Rachel.**

Another name that has followed two separate paths.

In England, it apparently is derived from a place name, which was also the family name of the nineteenth-century poet Percy Bysshe Shelley. His popularity led to its use as a given name, first for boys and more recently for girls. In the United States, it is usually regarded as a form of *Rachel*. Never a common name, it has gained strength since the 1950s. Actresses Shelley Duval, Shelley Winters.

### Shirley

Old English, "county meadow." Var: **Sherill, Sheryl, Shirl, Shirlee, Shirleen, Shirlene.**

Like *Evelyn* and a number of other names, this was given mainly to boys until the mid-nineteenth century, when it gradually became a preferred name for girls. The transition was assisted by the publication of Charlotte Brontë's novel *Shirley* (1849). Nearly one hundred years later, the fame of child actress Shirley Temple made it a favorite here. It has been in decline recently. Actress Shirley MacLaine; singer Shirley Bassey.

### Sibyl

Greek, "prophetess." Var: **Cybil, Cybill, Sibbie, Sibella, Sibelle, Sibilla, Sibylla, Sibylle, Sybil, Sybilla, Sybille.**

In ancient mythology the sibyls were women who could predict the future and who also assisted humans by interceding with the gods. The most famous sibyl was at Cumae, an early Greek colony in southern Italy. The name was brought from France to England by the Normans in the eleventh century; it was usually in fashion whenever classical Greek and Latin names were revived. It had a new rise in public appeal in the nineteenth century as the result of a novel, *Sybil* (1845), by Benjamin Disraeli, who later became British prime minister. The name is not connected with *Cybele*, from the name of a Greek and Roman fertility goddess and protectress of cities. Actress Cybill Shepherd.

## Stephanie

Greek, "crown." Var: **Stefanie, Steffi, Steffie, Stephana, Stephane.** See also the masculine **Stephen.**

The history of this name has been similar to that of *Michelle*. Never a familiar name until earlier in this century, it was adopted as the French feminine version of a popular masculine name. Since its introduction it has moved rapidly up the list, and it has been among the top ten for the past decade. TV newswoman Stephanie Shelton; actress Stefanie Powers.

## Susan

Hebrew, "lily." Var: **Sue, Susana, Susanna, Susannah, Susanne, Susi, Susie, Susy, Suzanna, Suzanne, Suzette, Suzi, Suzie, Suzy.**

As a personal rather than a flower name, it appeared first in the Book of Daniel, but the story of Susannah was not accepted as authentic by Jewish authorities on the Old Testament and is among the books of the Apocrypha. The name is also mentioned in the Gospel of Luke. Different forms have been given in England since the Middle Ages, but it was only after the Protestant Reformation of the sixteenth century that it entered common use. By the eighteenth century the shorter *Susan* was popular, along with diminutives such as *Sukey* and *Suky*, which are no longer seen. It fell off somewhat in the nineteenth century, then returned to become a favorite name in the 1950s. Actresses Susannah York, Suzanne Pleshette; columnist Suzy Parker.

## — T —

### Tamara

Hebrew, "palm tree." Var: **Tamar, Tammi, Tammie, Tammy.**

The palm tree has always been particularly valued in Mediterranean countries as a sign of water and life. Like the olive and laurel, the palm is also a traditional symbol of high honors, as well as of victory and peace. In the Old Testament, Tamar was the name of a daughter of King David and the sister of Absalom. The Russian *Tamara* and other forms have been adopted more frequently in the past half-century. Actress Tammy Grimes.

### Tanya

Greek, "sun." Var: **Tanyha, Tania, Titania.**

The Titans were ancient Greek gods defeated by Zeus, the king of gods. The word originally meant "sun" or "day," but the meaning of "giant" is now established because of the physical characteristics of the Titans. Titania was the name given by Shakespeare to the queen of the fairies in *A Midsummer Night's Dream*. As an alternative definition, the name has been traced to a Russian word possibly meaning "friend." Country singer Tanya Tucker.

### Teresa

Greek, "from Thera." Var: **Tera, Terese, Teresita, Teressa, Teri, Terri, Terry, Tess, Tessa, Tessi, Tessie, Tessy, Theresa, Therese.** See also **Tracy.**

Thera and the smaller Therasia are neighboring Greek islands in the Aegean. Despite its origin, the name is now regarded as Spanish because it first appeared in Spain about the sixth century. It was introduced into other countries only in the sixteenth century, with the veneration of a Spanish saint and Carmelite nun, Teresa of Avila. A nineteenth-century French saint, Therese of Lisieux, became famous as "the little flower." Another form gained attention in the past century with Thomas Hardy's novel *Tess of the D'Urbervilles*, made into a film in the late 1970s. Actresses Teresa Wright, Teri Garr.

## Tiffany

Greek, "divine manifestation." Var: **Tiff, Tiffi, Tiffie, Tiffy.**

This is a name from the Middle Ages that has taken wing in the last fifteen years. Probably most parents who have chosen it are unaware that it is from *Theophane*, a saint's name, which became *Tifaine* in France and later *Tiffany*, a family name in both France and England. The word also means a kind of thin gauze and a form of colored glass, made by Louis Tiffany, that first became fashionable in the early 1900s.

## Tracy

Greek, "from Thera." Var: **Trace, Tracey, Tracie.**
See **Teresa.** Generally defined as a contraction of the original name, but it may also come from a family name that was originally a French place name. Although *-ey* was ordinarily used for girls, no distinction between the two is made now. Tennis star Tracy Austin.

# Trudy

Old German, "strength." Var: **Trude, Trudie.**

This is a short form of *Gertrude*, an old name that is seldom used today. *Trudy* has stayed on a bit longer.

## — U —

# Una

Irish, "lamb." Var: **Ona, Oona, Unagh.**

An old Irish name, it has become better known as a derivation from the Latin word for one. It was used in this sense by the sixteenth-century poet Edmund Spenser in his *Faerie Queen*, but it still survives as an Irish name. It has never been common here, and so far it does not figure in the current revival of names from Ireland. Oona O'Neill Chaplin, daughter of playwright Eugene O'Neill, was married to the great silent-film comedian Charles Chaplin.

# Ursula

Latin, "little she bear." Var: **Ursa, Ursala, Ursella, Ursulina, Ursuline.**

According to legend, she was a fifth-century princess in Cornwall who was martyred and later canonized. Her name was taken by the Ursulines, a teaching order of nuns. The name was popular in the Middle Ages and was revived in the nineteenth century, but it is seldom given now. Actress Ursula Andress.

# — V —

## Valerie

Latin, "healthy." Var: **Val, Valeria, Valery, Valrie.**
Originally a French name, it was introduced in England and the United States only in the nineteenth century. (*Valentine*, both the name and the word, comes from the same root.) It has maintained a fairly steady popularity over the past fifty years. Actress Valerie Perrine.

## Vanessa

Latin, "class of butterfly." Var: **Nessa, Nessie, Van, Vann, Vanni, Vanny.**
This name is celebrated for its literary association. The eighteenth-century writer Jonathan Swift, wrongly believed to have invented *Stella* (see **Estelle**), actually did create *Vanessa* for another young woman friend. Oddly enough, both young women were named Esther. It was later given to a type of butterfly. Actress Vanessa Redgrave.

## Vera

Russian, "faith." Var: **Vere, Verina, Verine, Veria.**
Another possible root is the Latin word meaning "true." It has been a familiar name in Russia for many centuries, but it has only been used in English since the early 1900s.

## Veronica

Latin, "true image." Var: **Ronnie, Ronny, Veronika, Veronique.**

According to legend, when Jesus was carrying the cross to Calvary, a woman named Veronica defied the guards and wiped his bleeding face. The image said to be preserved on the cloth has been kept at St. Peter's in Rome since the eighth century. *Veronica* was popular in America in the 1940s (film star Veronica Lake), but is not often seen today.

## Victoria

Latin, "victory." Var: **Vicki, Vickie, Vicky, Viki, Vikki.**

The first Victoria was said to be a Roman martyr of the third century. Although sometimes given since the Middle Ages, the name never became well known until the reign of Queen Victoria, which spanned a major part of the nineteenth century. Her name was given to many things, including the era of her reign, but for some reason the name itself never became a favorite of parents at the time. It attained some popularity in the World War II period. Actress Victoria Principal; singer Vikki Carr.

## Violet

Latin, "violet plant." Var: **Vi, Viola, Violante, Violetta, Violette.** See also **Yolanda.**

Most flower names became popular about one hundred years ago, but this name is much older. It was fashionable in France and England in the late Middle Ages, and it was adopted by poets and authors of the Elizabethan era, including Shakespeare. A different form, *Yolanda*, is more familiar now. Dancer Violette Verdy.

## Virginia

Latin, "maiden." Var: **Ginni, Ginnie, Ginny, Jinny, Virginie.**

It has also been linked to *Virginius*, a Roman clan name, and an early Virginia was supposedly the martyred daughter of a Roman centurion. However, it received attention mainly from the decision by Sir Walter Raleigh to name the first permanent American colony Virginia, after Queen Elizabeth I, the "virgin queen." It has had regular periods of popularity here since the eighteenth century, but at the moment it is not often seen. Author Virginia Woolf.

# — W —

## Wanda

Old German, "kindred." Var: **Wenda, Wandie.**

Sometimes given as a form of *Gwendolen*, this name has an alternative origin from an Old English word meaning "wanderer," but the Germanic root seems more likely. It was occasionally found in the United States in the early 1900s; today it is unusual.

## Wilhelmina

Old German, "resolute guardian." Var: **Billi, Billie, Mina, Minna, Minnie, Velma, Vilma, Wilhelmine, Willa, Willamina, Willetta, Willi, Willie, Willy, Wilma, Wilmetta, Wylma.**

The original form of this name, from the German for *William*, is rarely used now. Shorter versions have sometimes been popular in the United States and have occasionally received considerable attention because of famous women athletes. Tennis star Billie Jean King; Olympic runner Wilma Rudolph, gold medalist in 1960.

## Winifred

Welsh, "blessed reconciliation." Var: **Freda, Wyn, Win, Winnie, Winny.**

The origin of this name is often confused with that of *Guinevere* and several others, perhaps because of a difficulty the English had in pronouncing Welsh names. They finally merged it with a similar-sounding Old English name that bore the meaning "friend of peace." Thus a *Winifred*—there aren't many today—can choose either definition. The name made slow progress from the Middle Ages onward, but it attained some fashion in this country in the early 1900s.

# — X —

## Xaviera

Arabic, "bright." Var: **Xaviere.**

A remnant of the Moorish conquest of Spain, it is the feminine of *Xavier*, more often given to boys.

# — Y —

## Yolanda

Latin, "violet plant." Var: **Iolande, Iolanthe, Yolande.**

See **Violet**. This version of the name is from a French form that developed during the Middle Ages. It is more familiar than the original today.

## Yvonne

Old French, "archer." Var: **Evonne, Yvette.**

Both *Yvonne* and *Yvette* are feminine forms of the French *Yves*, and although they are popular in France, only *Yvonne* has become well known in the United States and England. It was fashionable around the 1950s but has declined since then.

## — Z —

## Zelda

Old German, "battle maiden." Var: **Selda.**

This is probably the only form of *Griselda* still seen, and even this form is unusual nowadays. *Griselda* is an old name from the medieval era appearing in Chaucer's *Canterbury Tales*, and it was used later on for a witch and a cat (often a witch's companion). The shorter *Zelda* is known now primarily as the name of author F. Scott Fitzgerald's wife, Zelda Sayre, a model for many of his heroines (see **Nicole**).

## Zoe

Greek, "life." Var: **Zoa.** See also **Eve.**

When the Old Testament was translated into Greek in Alexandria about the time of Jesus, the Hebrew word for the name *Eve* was equated with the Greek word for life. Since Greek was the common language throughout the eastern part of the Roman empire, this name rather than *Eve* became a favorite in that area of the world. However, it was seldom seen in the West until the nineteenth century, and it has never been a favorite in the United States. Actress Zoe Caldwell.

# 9. Names for Boys

Variants, pet forms, and diminutives are listed under the major name heading. For a complete list of names, see the index.

## — A —

**Aaron**

Hebrew, "enlightened" or "shining." Var: **Aharon, Aron, Haroun, Harun.**

A biblical name whose popularity has recently been renewed. Aaron was the older brother of Moses, and since he was born during the Israelite bondage in Egypt, it has also been suggested that his name may be derived from an Egyptian word meaning "mountain." It appears in Arabic as *Haroun* and similar spellings. Because he was a more gifted speaker than his brother, Aaron was designated by God as Moses' prophet and as the first Hebrew high priest. Together they led their people out of bondage.

In the United States presidential election of 1800, Aaron Burr of New York and Thomas Jefferson of Virginia received an equal number of electoral votes. Jefferson was elected by the House of Representatives, and Burr became vice-president. Blaming Alexander Hamilton for this and other defeats, Burr fatally wounded him in a duel in 1804.

## Abraham

Hebrew, "father of a multitude." Var: **Abe, Abram, Avram, Bram.**

As described in the Book of Genesis, the founder of the Hebrew people was originally named Abram, but his name was changed at God's word: "Neither shall thy name any more be called Abram, but thy name shall be Abraham; for a father of many nations have I made thee." As a result of the high respect in which Abraham was held, his name was set aside for many centuries. Even when it reappeared, it was limited mainly to Jewish families until the time of the Protestant Reformation in the sixteenth century.

There was a similar revival of Old Testament names in this country in the late eighteenth century. Probably the best-known beneficiary was Abraham Lincoln, sixteenth president. A variation of the name is shown by Bram Stoker, an Irish novelist who wrote the classic *Dracula* (1897).

## Adam

Hebrew, "red earth." Var: **Ad, Adamo, Addie, Addy.**

As the first masculine name in the Bible, it is one of the oldest recorded names in history. Perhaps because of Adam's fall from grace and banishment from the garden of Eden, it was seldom used by Hebrew families, although there are later biblical references to cities that have similar names. However, as a Christian name, it was widespread in England and Scotland during the Middle Ages and until the eighteenth century. It has reappeared periodically since then and has been having a revival since the 1970s. After the original, the most famous bearer of the name may still be Adam Smith, Scottish author of *The Wealth of Nations* (1776), a pioneering work on the free marketplace that was important in shaping the American economy after the Revolution.

## Alan

Breton, "harmony." Var: **Al, Alain, Allan, Allen, Allie, Allyn.**

A Celtic name found very early in England, it apparently died out and was introduced a second time in the eleventh century after the Norman Conquest, when many settlers from Brittany arrived. At first it retained the French form, *Alain*, then became *Allan*, as in Allan-a-Dale, the minstrel companion of Robin Hood. It was especially popular in England in the nineteenth century and a bit later in the United States, during the early decades of this century; it reached a peak around the 1950s with the popularity of movie stars such as Alan Ladd. Still a familiar name among actors: Alan Alda, Alan Arkin. Astronaut Alan Shepard, first American in space (1961).

## Albert

Old German, "noble brilliance." Var: **Al, Alberto, Albie, Albrecht, Bert, Bertie, Elbert.**

This name took root in England first in tribute to Ethelbert, a sixth-century king who helped to convert the island to Christianity. After the eleventh century it took Latin and French forms (*Albertus* and *Aubert*), then grad-

ually declined in favor while retaining its popularity for
many centuries in Germany as *Albrecht*. The great revival
of the name in England occurred after Queen Victoria
married Prince Albert of Germany in 1840. A popular
figure, he was memorialized by many public buildings,
including the Royal Albert Hall and the Albert Memorial.

For several decades of the twentieth century, two men
were responsible for gaining the name worldwide attention. German-born American scientist Albert Einstein,
who formulated the theory of relativity, received the Nobel Prize for physics in 1921. Albert Schweitzer of France,
African missionary and doctor, won the Nobel Peace
Prize in 1952.

### Alexander

Greek, "protector of mankind." Var: **Al, Alec, Ale-
jandro, Alessandro, Alex, Alexio, Alexis, Lex, Sander,
Sandor, Sandro, Sandy, Sasha.** See also **Alistair.**

Going back some three thousand years in the Middle
East, it became a hereditary name among the kings of
Macedonia in Greece. Alexander the Great made it famous with his military conquests in the fourth century
B.C., giving the name to many cities, notably Alexandria
in Egypt, one of the leading centers of culture and learn-
ing in the ancient world. It was chosen by eight popes
and became a favorite with royal families, especially in
Eastern Europe. It was introduced into Scotland about
the twelfth century and within the next one hundred years
was the name of three kings; it has always been more
popular there than in England, so that *Sandy* came to
designate all Scotsmen. Actor Sir Alec Guinness; Pulitzer
Prize-winner (1977) Alex Haley, author of *Roots*.

## Alfred

Old English, "elf counsel." Var: **Al, Alf, Alfie, Alfredo, Fred, Fredo.** See also **Avery.**

The elves, now considered fairy-tale creatures, were regarded as wise spirits of nature in Anglo-Saxon culture, and this name element was often used in combined forms. Alfred the Great, a Saxon king of the late ninth century, was renowned as a lawgiver, scholar, statesman, and defender of his country against invaders from Denmark. Like most Old English names, it gradually disappeared after the Norman Conquest, but it returned in the nineteenth century when Alfred, Lord Tennyson was poet laureate. A later Englishman helped to bring it to attention in this country: Hollywood director Alfred Hitchcock.

## Alistair

Greek, "protector of mankind." Var: **Alastair, Alaster, Aleister, Alister, Allister.**

See **Alexander.** This version of the name, spelled in many different ways, has been popular in Scotland for centuries. Its adoption in England began about one hundred years ago, and recently it has been taken up by young American parents. Author and TV personality Alistair Cooke.

## Andrew

Greek, "manly." Var: **Anders, Andre, Andreas, Andrei, Andres, Andros, Andy, Drew, Dru.**

According to the New Testament, the brothers Andrew and Simon Peter were the first two apostles chosen by Jesus. Legend says that after the death of Jesus, Andrew became a missionary to the Balkan countries and was martyred in Greece on an X-shaped cross, now known as a St. Andrew's cross. Early in the Middle Ages, relics reported to be those of St. Andrew were brought to Scotland, and in this way his name was linked to that country and his emblem used for the Scottish national flag. The name gained ground more slowly in England, and it was not until 1960, when the current Prince Andrew was born, that it was chosen officially as a first name in the British royal family.

It was the name of the seventh and seventeenth United States presidents. Andrew Jackson, elected in 1828, was the founder of the Democratic party. Andrew Johnson was the vice-president who succeeded Abraham Lincoln in 1865. Johnson is the only president who was both impeached by the House of Representatives and tried (and eventually acquitted) by the Senate. Andrew Carnegie, the founder of U.S. Steel, gave financial support to libraries across the country.

The name continues to be popular today, with examples from many different fields: TV commentator and columnist Andy Rooney; composer and conductor Andre Previn; baseball star Andre Dawson.

### Anthony

Latin, "beyond price." Var: **Antoine, Anton, Antonin, Antonio, Antony, Tony.**

Originally a Roman clan name, it first gained attention because of Mark Antony, or Marcus Antonius, the close friend of Julius Caesar and lover of Cleopatra, queen of Egypt; all three are also major characters in plays by Shakespeare. Later it was the name of several saints venerated during the Middle Ages, especially the Franciscan friar Antony of Padua.

The spelling *Anthony*, found mainly in English-speaking countries, was adopted about the sixteenth century. In England, however, it is still generally pronounced without the "h." Actors Anthony Quinn, Tony Curtis.

## Arnold

Old German, "eagle power." Var: **Arn, Arnie, Arnaldo, Arnaud, Arnoldo.**

A name that was apparently brought to England in the eleventh century, it took a number of forms but never achieved great popularity. For several hundred years it survived as a family name; by the late nineteenth century, due to a number of prominent people such as poet Matthew Arnold, it slowly began to influence first names again. Golf champion Arnold Palmer.

## Arthur

Welsh, "bear hero." Var: **Art, Arte, Artie, Artur, Arturo, Arty.**

As a result of the enduring Camelot legend, *Arthur* was one of the most celebrated names to emerge from the medieval period. Under the circumstances it is not surprising that explanations vary regarding its origin; since most of them involve a word element meaning "bear," a symbol of strength and courage, this explanation may be the most appropriate.

Although there seems to have been an actual King Arthur in the late eighth century, historians were divided until recently as to whether or not the adventures of Arthur and his Knights of the Round Table represent largely fiction or fact. A principal reason for doubt is that most of the Arthurian tales were translated from French, based on familiar stories embodying the medieval concept of chivalry. The romances of the Middle Ages were widely known throughout Western Europe and the British Isles; each country had its own heroes and borrowed or adapted freely the stories from other lands. Nevertheless, there is general agreement now that some historical basis exists for the adventures of an English Arthur, whose court was probably somewhere in the Cornwall region.

There have been many versions of the Arthurian legend. The most recent to reach a wide audience was *Camelot*, a musical play and film of the 1960s from a book by T. H. White (*The Once and Future King*). Probably the most influential has been Alfred, Lord Tennyson's *Idylls of the King*, a series of poetic romances that began appearing in 1859. His work helped to revive many of the old medieval names found in the tales of the Round Table.

Playwright Arthur Miller; concert pianist Artur Rubinstein; actor Arte Johnson; humorist Art Buchwald.

## Avery

Old English, "elf counsel." Var: **Ave.**

See **Alfred.** The original name was spelled in several different written forms, one of which became *Avery*; recently it has been used in some places for girls as well as for boys. It should not be confused with *Averell*, a name that has another Old English root ("boar battle"). Novelist Avery Corman's *Kramer vs. Kramer* was made into an Academy Award-winning movie (1979).

# — B —

## Barnaby

Aramaic, "son of consolation." Var: **Barn, Barnabas, Barney, Barnie.**

Like a number of names in the New Testament, it comes from a language spoken in the Middle East about the time of the Roman occupation. Some researchers suggest that the key element in the name is "exhortation," but the definition given above is commonly accepted. The first Barnabas was a companion of Paul the Apostle on his early journeys around the Mediterranean. The name has never been given widely in England or in the United States, but from time to time it has been a favorite of authors. Charles Dickens' novel *Barnaby Rudge* (1841); the recent TV series *Barnaby Jones* and *Barney Miller*.

## Barry

Irish, "spear thrower." Var: **Bar, Barrie.**

This is sometimes assumed to be a variation of other names beginning with the *bar-* element, but it is in fact an old Celtic name that gained favor mainly in Ireland. Until the nineteenth century it seldom appeared elsewhere, but by the 1950s it had become a familiar choice of American families. Senator Barry Goldwater; singer Barry Manilow.

## Bartholomew

Aramaic, "son of Talmai." Var: **Bart, Barthel, Barthelmy, Bartie, Bartle, Bartlett, Bartolomeo, Bartley.**

The root of this New Testament name means "furrow," so it probably has some relation to farming. In the first three Gospels, Bartholomew is named as one of the original twelve apostles, but in the Gospel of John the name of Nathaniel appears instead; it has been suggested that both names refer to the same person. The name was popular in the Middle Ages and was given to one of the first hospitals founded in England, St. Bartholomew's of London.

## Benjamin

Hebrew, "son of the right hand." Var: **Ben, Benji, Benjy, Benn, Benny.**

As described in the Book of Genesis, Benjamin was the youngest brother of Joseph and the last-born son of Rachel and Jacob. His mother, who died after his difficult birth, called him *Ben-Oni*, or "son of sorrow," but Jacob changed his name to mean that the boy was a blessed or favorite child, an unexpected gift from God. It was one of the Old Testament names revived by the Puritans in the sixteenth century. Its major influence in this country was undoubtedly due to the prominence of Benjamin Franklin, statesman, author, and inventor. Benjamin Harrison, elected in 1888, was the twenty-third president. Baby doctor Benjamin Spock; musician Benny Goodman.

## Bernard

Old German, "bear courage." Var: **Barnard, Barney, Barnie, Bern, Bernardo, Berne, Bernhard, Bernie, Berny.**

Like *Arthur*, this is another medieval name symbolically linked to the bear. Two friars of the eleventh and twelfth centuries made the name famous. Bernard of Menthon was the monk who established hospices for travelers in the Alps, along two passes that became known as the Great and Little St. Bernard. The well-known dogs that sought out voyagers lost in the snow were also named after him, although they were added several centuries later. Bernard of Clairvaux was a founder of the Cistercian order, a famous writer and preacher, and an adviser to popes and kings. The name declined in popularity after the Protestant Reformation but returned in the nineteenth century.

Playwright George Bernard Shaw (who was never called George); novelist Bernard Malamud.

## Bradford

Old English, "broad crossing." Var: **Brad.**

A place name and family name, similar to *Bradley* ("broad meadow"), given by parents increasingly as a first name. Actor Bradford Dillman.

## Brendan

Irish, "sword." Var: **Bran, Brand, Brandon, Brandt, Brant, Bren, Brend, Brenden, Brennan, Brent, Brenton.**

The two names *Brandon* and *Brendan* are given different origins by some authors, based on the assumption that the first derives from an Old English word meaning "torch." It seems likely, however, that they represent English and Irish variations on the name of a sixth-century Irish monk who established a monastery at Clonfert that lasted for over one thousand years. But he became better known as a voyager when, several centuries after his death, tales were circulated in many languages describing his expedition to an island of paradise somewhere in the West. According to legend, Columbus was familiar with these stories and was influenced by them to sail in a western direction in search of the Indies.

Author and playwright Brendan Behan. Actor Brandon de Wilde played the role of the young farmboy in the film classic *Shane* (1953).

## Brett

Old French, "Breton." Var: **Bret, Brit, Britt.**

The Bretons, from the French region of Brittany across the Channel from England, migrated to Ireland and Scotland many centuries before the Christian era. Julius Caesar associated them with tribes on the mainland because of the similarity of language and culture; he called

the islands Britain. Initially a family name, it came
into use as a first name during the past century. Bret Harte,
nineteenth-century author and poet, wrote many tales of
the American frontier.

## Brian

Irish, "strong." Var: **Brien, Brion, Bryan, Bryant,
Bryon.**

Brian Boru was the first great king of Ireland, who
defeated a Danish force early in the eleventh century.
But the name was probably brought to England in the
same century after the Norman invasion, by a new wave
of settlers from Brittany. It was popular in different forms
during the Middle Ages, then declined until the 1700s.
After a brief revival, it went out of fashion again in
England, but it remained a favorite in Ireland and was
brought to the United States in the nineteenth century by
Irish immigrants. Currently it is on most lists of preferred
names. Actor Brian Keith; TV anchorman Bryant Gumbel.

## Broderick

Welsh, "son of Roderick." Var: **Brod, Broddie.**

See **Roderick.** It probably represents a Welsh variation
on a name popular in Scotland. Actor Broderick Crawford.

## Bruce

Old French, "from Brieuse." Var: **Brucie.**

Although this name is often considered to be typically
Scottish, it is probably another example of a Breton name
that arrived in the British Isles as a result of the Norman
Conquest of the eleventh century. Apparently the branch
of the family that developed in Scotland proved to be

more active, because Robert Bruce later became the country's great national hero when he defeated the English armies in 1314. Use of the family name as a first name began in Scotland as a result of his victories. The name has periodically been a favorite in the United States since the nineteenth century. Singer Bruce Springsteen.

## Burton

Old English, "hill town." Var: **Burt, Burte.**

Spelled *Bert*, the name is usually a form of longer names that include this element as a beginning (*Bertram*) or ending (*Albert*). In either case, the basic meaning is "brightness" or "brilliance." The substitution of a "u" indicates another origin. A principal town or borough (from *burg*) was often situated on a hill for purposes of defense and was well fortified. These concepts come together in a different version of the name. Actors Burt Lancaster, Burt Reynolds.

## Byron

Old French, "from Biron." Var: **Biron, Byrin.**

Another family name brought to the British Isles in the Norman invasion. It is one of those few names that are nearly always associated with an individual bearer, in this case the English poet George Gordon, Lord Byron, whose romantic verse and reputation won him instant fame in the early years of the nineteenth century. Supreme Court Justice Byron R. White.

# — C —

## Calvin

Latin, "bald." Var: **Cal, Calvie, Calvino.**

Before surnames were widely established, one of the common ways to identify members of a family was by associating them with a physical characteristic of a well-known ancestor, which didn't necessarily have to be complimentary. There was, in fact, a ninth-century king of France called Charles the Bald (*Calvinus*). A later descendant may well have been John Calvin, French religious reformer of the sixteenth century. Named directly for him was John Calvin Coolidge, the thirtieth United States president and so far the only president born on the Fourth of July (1872). Fashion designer Calvin Klein.

## Carey

Latin, "dear, costly." Var: **Cary.**

A family name of uncertain roots. It occurs in different regions of England, Scotland, and Ireland, and the original Latin meaning was affected in a variety of ways by its passage through Old English and the Celtic tongues. It has been used as a first name since the nineteenth century. Actor Cary Grant.

## Carl

Old German, "man." Var: **Carlo, Carlos, Carroll, Caryl, Karel, Karl.**

See **Charles.** During the Middle Ages, official records were kept in Latin, and whatever the actual form of this name, it usually appeared as *Carolus*. The Old English and French pronunciation, however, included an "h," so that later on *Charles* became the generally accepted spelling. But in Germany, the Scandinavian countries, Italy, and Spain, national versions of *Carl* have been familiar for many centuries. Immigrants to the United States gave it a popularity that rivaled that of *Charles* until the 1960s, when both names began to lose favor with parents. Olympic track champion Carl Lewis; actor Karl Malden.

## Casey

Irish, "valorous." Var: **Case.**

This family name from Ireland has been given as a first name and nickname for boys for at least one hundred years in the United States. More recently it has occasionally been used for girls. Long-time baseball manager Casey Stengel.

## Charles

Old German, "man." Var: **Charley, Charlie, Chaz, Chick, Chuck.** See also **Carl, Charlton.**

This name was made famous early in the Middle Ages by two leaders of the Franks, later the French. Charles Martel (Charles the Hammer) commanded the forces that defeated Saracen armies at Tours in 732, the farthest point reached in the Arab invasion of Europe. His grandson Charlemagne (Charles the Great) was crowned Holy Roman Emperor on Christmas Day, 800, in Rome. The title lasted for one thousand years, although the territory it covered became progressively smaller with the passage of time. In Charlemagne's day it included France, Germany, and regions of Austria, Italy, and Spain. His reign is noted for its civilizing influence and strong support of Christianity. More than thirty-five rulers of European countries subsequently had the name, with the largest number concentrated in France and Sweden.

A different history has prevailed in Britain, where there have been only two kings named Charles. The first was deposed (and executed) in 1649 by Parliament and the Puritan leader Oliver Cromwell; the second, his son, died without leaving a legitimate heir. When the current Prince Charles succeeds to the throne, he will be the first British sovereign of that name in three hundred years. No American president has ever had *Charles* as a first name. Nevertheless, it has remained a favorite name among families, reaching a peak in the nineteenth century.

Three famous Englishmen from diverse fields: Charles Darwin, the naturalist who first described the theory of evolution; novelist Charles Dickens; film comedian Charles Chaplin. Probably the best-known native *Charles* is still Charles Lindbergh, who made the first solo transatlantic flight in 1927.

## Charlton

Old English, "farmers' town." Var: **Carlton, Carleton.**

See **Charles.** Because of its prevalence in the countryside, the name took on a rustic character in England, denoting a peasant or farmer. Some rural villages and towns were named in this way. This meaning does not apply to American cities like Charleston, South Carolina, which was named directly for Charles II. Actor Charlton Heston.

## Christian

Latin, "follower of Christ." Var: **Chris, Christie, Christy, Kris, Kristian.** See also the feminine **Christina.**

The feminine version of the name, from that of an early martyr and saint, evolved about the same time as the masculine but has always been more widely used. It has been a popular name for boys in only a few countries, such as France and Denmark, where ten Danish kings have been called *Christian*. Fashion designer Christian Dior.

## Christopher

Greek, "bearer of Christ." Var: **Chris, Christie, Christy, Christoph, Cris, Cristoforo, Kit, Kris, Kristy.**

There are several saints with this name, but the first and best known (as the patron of travelers) was a third-century martyr. According to legend, he was a physically powerful man who lived by a river and helped people to cross over. One stormy night as he bore a small boy on his shoulders, he discovered that he was carrying the Christ child. He was widely venerated during the medieval era, and his name remained a favorite even after the Protestant Reformation. Christopher Marlowe was the leading English playwright before Shakespeare, and the seventeenth-century architect Christopher Wren designed many of the famous churches in London.

The name has a special significance for Americans because of Christopher Columbus. A holiday in most states, Columbus Day commemorates his first sighting of land in what is now the Bahamas. Although it was in decline earlier, *Christopher* has been revived by today's parents. Actor and singer Kris Kristofferson; rodeo champion Chris Lybbert.

## Clark

Latin, "cleric." Var: **Clarke, Clarkie.**

In medieval Latin this term described a minor clergyman who had the responsibility of making and keeping records. Eventually, it came to mean anyone who performed similar work in a shop or office. In England both the occupation and the name are pronounced in the same way, but Americans say them differently. It has only become a first name within the past one hundred years. Actor Clark Gable.

## Clement

Latin, "merciful." Var: **Clem, Clemens, Clemente, Clemmie.**

Clement appears in the New Testament as a colleague of the Apostle Paul, and it was also the name of the fourth bishop of Rome; the two may be the same person. The legend of Clement's martyrdom is that he was tied to an anchor and thrown into the sea; thus he became a patron of seafarers. The name has had occasional periods of fashion in the United States, but it is more common in England, where Clement Attlee became prime minister at the end of World War II.

## Clifford

Old English, "crossing by the cliff." Var: **Cliff, Cliffie, Clive.**

From an English place name. There seems to be little trace of it as a first name until the nineteenth century, but it has become increasingly popular in the past fifty years. Playwright Clifford Odets; actor Cliff Robertson.

## Clinton

Old English, "headland town." Var: **Clint.**

Another place name that became an English family name and then, much more recently, a first name favored in the United States. As governor of New York in the early nineteenth century, DeWitt Clinton was responsible for developing the Erie Canal. Actor Clint Eastwood.

## Colin

Scottish, "cub, puppy." Var: **Cole, Collin, Colum, Cullen.**

The definition given here seems a likely one because the name is popular in Scotland, where it has a long tradition in the Campbell family, one of the country's oldest clans. However, at least three other definitions have been suggested. It may have been brought to Britain by the Normans as an Old French form of *Nicholas*. There is also a similar name in Wales derived from the word for a hazel grove. Finally, the Irish name *Colum* or *Columba* comes from the Latin word for dove. The name was seldom seen in this country until pilot Colin Kelly became the first American hero of World War II.

## Craig

Scottish, "crag." Var: **Craigie, Craigy.**

A family name from Scotland that has been given as a first name, though not widely, since the late nineteenth century. Restaurant and food expert Craig Claiborne.

## Curtis

Old French, "courteous." Var: **Curt, Curtiss, Kurt.**

This is a paradoxical name in that its long and short forms are nearly opposite in their original meanings. Manners at court were supposed to be polite and gracious; someone who was courteous behaved as if in the presence of royalty. The family name Curtis comes out of this tradition. However, *Curt*, from the Latin "shorten," describes someone concise or abrupt in speech. Spelled

*Kurt*, it originated in German-speaking lands as a short form of *Konrad* ("bold counsel"). Novelist Kurt Vonnegut.

# — D —

## Dale

Old English, "valley." Var: **Dael.**

This old family name has had periods of popularity as a name for girls—a recent example is Dale Evans, western singer and entertainer with her husband, Roy Rogers. But throughout most of its history, it has been a masculine first name. Writer and lecturer Dale Carnegie (*How to Win Friends and Influence People*) established one of the first modern networks of confidence-building programs early in this century. Baseball star Dale Murphy.

## Damon

Greek, "subdue, tame." Var: **Damian, Damiano, Damien.**

In the fourth century B.C., Damon and Pythias were reportedly two friends in Sicily whose loyalty to each other made their names a byword for companionship. The name of Damon has continued in various forms through the centuries, but that of Pythias has been almost totally neglected. Damon Runyon's stories of Broadway life in the years before World War II formed the basis for the musical play and film of the 1950s *Guys and Dolls*.

## Dana

Scandinavian, "from Denmark." Var: **Dane**. See also the feminine **Dana**.

Danish invasions were a major problem in England and neighboring countries from the ninth to the eleventh century. The presence of Danish settlements also influenced the development of native languages. Actor Dana Andrews.

## Daniel

Hebrew, "God is my judge." Var: **Dan, Dannie, Danny**.

Some of the classic scenes in the Old Testament appear in the Book of Daniel, the captive Hebrew prophet who interpreted the dreams of the king of Babylon. Daniel was cast into a lions' den for refusing to deny his religion, but with God's protection he emerged unharmed. It was also Daniel who interpreted the famous "handwriting on the wall," predicting the coming downfall of the Babylonian kingdom.

The name entered general use about the twelfth century, was taken up by the Puritans, and became a great favorite in the eighteenth and nineteenth centuries. Frontiersman Daniel Boone and celebrated orator Daniel Webster were only two of the many Americans to bear the name. Its popularity declined for several generations, but it gradually returned and is once again a preferred name.

## Darren

Irish, "great." Var: **Daren, Darin, Darrin**.

This is only one suggested meaning; others include both English and French place names. It may also be distantly related to *Dorian* (see the feminine **Doris**). An

unusual name that has gained attention in recent years.
Actor Darren McGavin.

## David

Hebrew, "beloved." Var: **Dave, Davie, Davis, Davit, Davy.**

Like *Daniel*, here is another biblical name that seems
to be achieving a new peak of popularity. The life of
David, second king of Israel, receives detailed attention
in the Old Testament, extending through four books; he
is also generally accepted as the author of approximately
half of the 150 hymns in the Book of Psalms. Many of
his exploits are familiar, including his victory over the
giant Goliath, the rivalry with King Saul, his reign as
king when the capital was established at Jerusalem, and
his death early in the tenth century B.C., followed by the
reign of his son Solomon. The Star of David is the national emblem of Israel.

It is an old name in the British Isles, where St. David
is the patron of Wales and two early Scottish kings were
named David. One of the best-known English novels is
Charles Dickens' *David Copperfield* (1849), and David
Lloyd George was British prime minister during World
War I. Generations of children here and abroad have
grown up with the adventures of Davy Crockett, who
died defending the Alamo in 1836.

## Dennis

Greek, "of Dionysus." Var: **Denis, Dennie, Denny, Denys, Denison, Dion.**

Dionysus, also known as Bacchus, was the god of
grapes and wine. Despite its place in Greek and Roman
mythology, this name has a long Christian tradition as
well; as described in the New Testament, Dionysius was

a member of the Athenian tribunal who was converted by Paul the Apostle. It appeared later in Old French as Denys, a third-century martyr in Paris who became the patron of France. The name was brought by the Normans to England, but it was less popular there than in Ireland, and the Irish form *Dennis* is the most common in the United States. Actor Dennis Weaver.

## Derek

Old German, "ruler of the people." Var: **Darrick, Derrick, Deryk, Dirk.**

This medieval name traveled from Germany to Britain via Belgium. Except as a family name, it seems to have declined after the seventeenth century, but it was revived in the early 1900s. Author and poet Derek Walcott.

## Dominic

Latin, "of the Lord." Var: **Dom, Domenico, Domingo, Dominick, Nick, Nicky.**

Three major strands of tradition make up this name. Initially, it had the meaning "belonging to the Lord (Jesus)," but since Sunday is the Lord's day for Christians (*dies dominica*), it has also been used in naming if a birth or other important event took place on that day. The island of Dominica in the West Indies was so named by Columbus because it was discovered on a Sunday. Early in the thirteenth century, the Spanish St. Dominic founded an order of friars who soon became the leading teachers in Europe; many boys were named after him.

## Donald

Scottish, "world ruler." Var: **Don, Donal, Donnie, Donny.**

An old Gaelic name in Ireland and especially in Scotland, where it became firmly established as a first name and clan name (MacDonald). It enjoyed great popularity in the United States early in the present century, but it is not seen as often today. TV sportscaster Don Meredith; actor Donald Sutherland.

## Douglas

Scottish, "dark water." Var: **Doug, Dougie, Douglass.**
Another Gaelic name that found a favorable reception in Scotland, but unlike *Donald* it was a place and family name before it gained attention as a first name. It has been a fairly regular if not preferred choice of American parents since the 1800s. General Douglas MacArthur was a commander in the Pacific during World War II and the Korean War.

## Dustin

Old German, "brave fighter." Var: **Dust, Dustie, Dusty.**
The origin is uncertain. It may also be derived from the Old English *Dunstan*, meaning "hill stone." Another possibility is that it is a formal rendering of the nickname *Dusty*, often associated with the occupation (and then family name) of "miller" in the Middle Ages. Today it is known primarily because of the actor Dustin Hoffman, but there was a cowboy star named Dustin Farnum in the silent-movie era.

## Dylan

Welsh, "son of the wave." Var: **Dill, Dillan.**
The name of a legendary Welsh hero, it was seldom seen in this country until the 1970s. Its appearance may partly be explained by the popularity of singer and composer Bob Dylan. Poet Dylan Thomas, author of the holiday classic *A Child's Christmas in Wales*.

# ___ E ___

## Earl

Old English, "nobleman." Var: **Earle, Erle, Errol.**

In the British nobility an earl is in the middle rank, below a duke and marquis and above a viscount and baron; in other countries the title corresponds to count. It has hardly ever been used as a first name in Britain, but in the United States it made a strong run in the first decades of this century. It may be having a slight revival. Football star Earl Campbell; mystery writer Erle Stanley Gardner, creator of the lawyer-detective Perry Mason; actor Errol Flynn.

## Edgar

Old English, "spear of prosperity." Var: **Edgard.** See also **Edward.**

Alphabetically the first of the four major *Ed-* names, based on an Anglo-Saxon word element conveying the idea of prosperity, riches, and possessions; it also includes a touch of happiness. This element formed part of the names of many of the Saxon kings who reigned from the ninth to the eleventh century. Only one was named Edgar, but he was the first to be accepted as ruler of all England. The name practically disappeared after the Norman Conquest, but it was revived in the nineteenth century.

Two famous American authors have had the name. Edgar Allan Poe's tales of terror are known throughout the world and have often been adapted for movies. Edgar Rice Burroughs was the creator of Tarzan, another staple of the film industry; the first Tarzan story was published

in 1913, and the first of an endless series of movies
appeared five years later.

## Edmund

Old English, "protector of prosperity." Var: **Eamon,
Edmond.** See also **Edward.**

England has had two royal saints; the first was King
Edmund, who was killed by Danish invaders in the ninth
century. (The second was Edward; see below.) Another
St. Edmund was Archbishop of Canterbury in the 1200s.
The name has never fallen out of fashion, but it also has
never been widely popular.

## Edward

Old English, "guardian of prosperity." Var: **Ed, Ed-
die, Eddy, Edouard, Eduardo, Edvard, Ned, Neddie,
Neddy, Ted, Teddie, Teddy.**

In terms of preference through the centuries, this has
always been the favorite among *Ed-* names. Since 1272,
when it was reestablished as a royal name in England,
there have been eight kings named Edward, the last of
whom abdicated in 1936 to marry an American. In the
twelfth century, Edward the Confessor became the second
of England's royal saints after the earlier Edmund. His
tomb is the central shrine in Westminster Abbey.

As in Britain, the name has remained a steady favorite
here, though its ranking is lower today than it was at
mid-century. Senator Edward M. Kennedy; playwright
Edward Albee, winner of two Pulitzer Prizes (1967, 1975).

## Edwin

Old English, "friend of prosperity." Var: **Edwyn.** See
also **Edward.**

The name of a seventh-century ruler in the northern

part of Britain who was converted to Christianity. According to legend, he was the founder of Scotland's capital, Edinburgh. Like *Edgar*, the name dropped from use after the Norman invasion but returned in the nineteenth century. With Neil Armstrong, astronaut Edwin Aldrin made the first lunar landing in 1969. Olympic track champion Edwin Moses.

## Eli

Hebrew, "height, elevation." Var: **Elie, Ely, Elye.**

This Old Testament name was later adopted as a short form of *Elijah* and *Elias*, but it originally had a different Hebrew root. A familiar name to students of American history because of Eli Whitney, inventor of the cotton gin (1793).

## Elijah

Hebrew, "Jehovah is God." Var: **Elia, Elias, Elihu.** See also **Elliott.**

Most of the story of Elijah, one of the great biblical prophets, appears in the First Book of Kings. To please the wicked Queen Jezebel, King Ahab introduced the worship of Baal. Elijah aroused the people against this idolatry and, after many struggles, both Ahab and Jezebel met a violent end. The Hebrew name was changed to *Elias* when it was written in Greek, and this version was taken for names through the Middle Ages. After the Protestant Reformation of the sixteenth century, *Elijah* was revived along with similar biblical names like *Eleazar* ("God is help"), also given as *Lazarus*, and *Elisha* ("God is salvation"), the name of the successor to the prophet Elijah. A number of these names were popular with American families in the nineteenth century; some have appeared again since the 1970s.

Elia Kazan, director of many stage and screen successes, among them the Academy Award-winning *On the Waterfront* (1954).

## Elliott

Old English, "son of Elias." Var: **Eliot, Elliot, Ellis.**
See **Elijah**. From an English form of the name that later became a family name. Since the late nineteenth century it has sometimes been given as a first name. Actor Elliott Gould.

## Emil

Old German, "industrious." Var: **Emile, Emiliano, Emilio, Emlin, Emlyn.**
It has been suggested that the original root comes from a Roman *gens* or clan name, *Aemilius*. Although the feminine *Emily* was very popular in the past century, the masculine form has never been widely used in English-speaking countries. As *Emlyn*, it has sometimes been chosen by Welsh families, but it may have had a different origin in that language.

## Eric

Scandinavian, "ruler." Var: **Erich, Erick, Erik.**
More specific definitions may be "ever-ruler" and "island-ruler." The Viking navigator Eric the Red discovered and named Greenland in the tenth century. He was the father of Leif Ericson, who is said to have been the first to discover North America. The name was seldom found in the United States until the nineteenth century, when settlers from Scandinavia made it familiar. It became fashionable around the 1920s, and it seems to be on the rise again. Skating star Eric Heiden.

## Ernest

Old German, "purposeful." Var: **Ern, Ernesto, Ernie, Ernst, Erny.**

Known in German-speaking lands since the Middle Ages, the name has been given outside those countries only since the 1800s. It was a favorite in some parts of the United States at the turn of the century, but its fortunes have declined since then. Author Ernest Hemingway was awarded a Nobel Prize in 1954.

## Ethan

Hebrew, "constancy." Var: **Ethe, Eythan.**

A biblical name revived by the Puritans, it apparently lasted longer on American shores, especially in New England, than it did in the mother country. Ethan Allen of the Green Mountain Boys in Vermont was a leader in the Revolutionary War. So far it hasn't benefited from the renewal of interest in Old Testament names.

## Eugene

Greek, "of noble birth." Var: **Eugen, Eugenio, Gene.** See also **Owen.**

Dating from at least the sixth century, this name has had periods of popularity in Europe and the British Isles ever since. Like *Ernest*, it was particularly favored in the United States around the turn of the century, and it has followed the same descending course. Playwright Eugene O'Neill, a Nobel Prize-winner in 1936, is the only author to have received four Pulitzer Prizes (1920, 1922, 1928, 1957).

## Evan

Hebrew, "God is gracious." Var: **Ev, Even, Evin.** See also **Owen.**

See **John**, of which this is usually taken to be a Welsh form. But like many Welsh names, it may also have a native meaning, which in this case is "young warrior." Evan Hunter is the author of the 1950s novel *The Blackboard Jungle*.

## Ezra

Hebrew, "help." Var: **Esdras, Esra, Ez.**

The Book of Ezra principally describes the career of this famous scholar and priest, whose importance in the Old Testament approaches that of Moses. In the fifth century B.C., it was Ezra who assumed responsibility for reviving Hebrew tradition after the captivity in Babylon. Another name taken up by the Puritans in the sixteenth century, it has retained the favor of a small percentage of parents through the years.

— F —

## Farley

Old English, "fair meadow." Var: **Fairleigh, Fairlie, Farleigh, Farlie, Farly, Farr.**

A family name taken from a place name. Unlike many other first names with the same ending (*Ashley, Beverly,* etc.), this one is still used almost exclusively, if not extensively, for boys. Actor Farley Granger.

### Fletcher

Old French, "maker of arrows." Var: **Fletch.**

Another old family name, from a respected medieval occupation. Composer-arranger Fletcher Henderson pioneered swing and dance bands in the 1930s.

### Floyd

Welsh, "gray." Var: **Floyde.**

See **Lloyd**, of which this is said to be a variation ("son of Lloyd"). Floyd Patterson twice won the heavyweight boxing championship (1956, 1960).

### Francis

Latin, "from France." Var: **Fran, Francesco, Franchot, Francisco, François, Frank, Frankie, Franky, Franz.** See also **Franklin.**

The name of the tribes known collectively as the Franks, who settled in the country that became France, originally meant "free" or "free men." Thus the short form *Frank* or something similar probably came before any longer version. However, the name had its first wave of popularity beginning in the thirteenth century because of Francis of Assisi, who founded the Franciscan order of friars and dedicated his life to poverty and the love of all God's creatures. Supposedly, this was not the name given by his mother, who had him baptized *Giovanni (John)* in his father's absence. There are two accounts of how the change occurred. His father, a wealthy cloth merchant who traveled between Italy and France, called him *Francesco* after returning home. Or later on, the name was bestowed by school friends because his clothes and manner gave him a French appearance.

In any case, many others subsequently received the

name during and after the Middle Ages, including the Spanish saint Francis Xavier and the French saint Francis de Sales. Active in the Elizabethan era were the navigator Francis Drake and the scholar and scientist Francis Bacon, periodically revealed as the "true" author of Shakespeare's plays. The name has had an up-and-down history in the United States, influenced by the alternative choice of *Franklin*; it seems to have been in decline since the 1950s.

## Franklin

Middle English, "freeholder." Var: **Francklyn, Franklyn.** See also **Francis.**

Although related to *Francis* in origin, this name had a separate meaning, designating a landowner whose property was freely held and not obtained through noble birth. It became popular in the United States as a tribute to Benjamin Franklin, a signer of the Declaration of Independence and one of the founders of the nation. It was the name of the fourteenth president, Franklin Pierce, and the thirty-second, Franklin D. Roosevelt, the only president to serve more than two terms in office.

## Frederick

Old German, "peaceful ruler." Var: **Federico, Federigo, Fred, Freddie, Freddy, Frederick, Frederik, Fredric, Fredrick, Friedrich, Fritz.**

Until the early eighteenth century, this name was found mainly in Germany. It was made famous by King Friedrich Barbarossa (Frederick the Red-Beard), who was reported in 1190 to have died in Turkey during the Third Crusade. The circumstances gave rise to the legend that he had not perished but was sleeping in a cave, ready to return at a moment of great danger. It was the name of six kings of Prussia, among them Frederick the Great in the eighteenth century, who laid the foundation of the German nation.

Although it had been known in England since the Middle Ages, the name became fashionable only in the 1700s. From that time its popularity began to grow in both England and America, reaching a high point early in this century. Novelist Frederick Forsyth; film director Federico Fellini; actor Fredric March, an Academy Award-winner for *The Best Years of Our Lives* (1946).

# ___ G ___

## Gabriel

Hebrew, "man of God." Var: **Gabe, Gabie, Gabriello.**

One of only two angels mentioned by name in both the Old and New Testaments (the other is Michael), Gabriel serves mainly as the bringer of good news. In the Gospel of Luke, he announces the coming birth of John the Baptist and of Jesus. As a first name, it has been more familiar in France and Italy than in English-speaking countries.

## Gary

Old German, "spear." Var: **Gari, Garey, Garry.**

See **Gerald**. This short form of the name may come from an Irish variation and family name. "Garryowen" is an old Irish ballad. The name became internationally known through the long career of movie star Gary Cooper.

# Gavin

Welsh, "little hawk." Var: **Gaven, Gawen.**

Today this is considered a Scottish name, although it goes far back in Welsh legend. An earlier form appears in *Sir Gawain and the Green Knight*, a fourteenth-century medieval tale of chivalry. *Gavin* is not often found in the United States.

# Geoffrey

Old German, "God's peace" or "country peace." Var: **Geoff.**

See **Jeffrey**, the spelling popular in America. Probably the best-known bearer of the name in this form is Geoffrey Chaucer, England's first major poet and author of *The Canterbury Tales* (approximately 1390).

# George

Greek, "farmer." Var: **Geordie, Georg, Georges, Georgie, Georgy, Giorgio, Jorge.**

According to legend, the first St. George was a Roman officer and Christian martyred in Palestine early in the fourth century. His story became familiar in Eastern churches, but it was only eight hundred years later that the crusaders learned about him. In time he grew to be an idealized hero of chivalry, the symbolic leader of an order of English knights, and by the 1400s the patron of England. Possibly his name was judged to be too special for ordinary use, but it was seldom found until the reign of the Hanover kings named George began in 1714. After that it gradually became one of the most common of English names.

King George III was roundly detested by the American colonists, and yet the name's popularity continued to increase after the Revolutionary War. The explanation can only be that the new nation now had its own leader named George, the first president and still the only one to have the name. As with Benjamin Franklin and Thomas Jefferson, both elements of George Washington's name have been given, either singly or together, by American parents to their children.

## Gerald

Old German, "spear ruler." Var: **Garald, Garold, Geraldo, Geraud, Gerold, Gerry, Giraldo, Jerrold, Jerry.** See also **Gary.**

Both this name and the similar *Gerard* ("spear courage") have been known in Britain since the Norman Conquest, and the latter form was more commonly used for several centuries. But *Gerald* survived, possibly because of the powerful Irish family Fitzgerald of Kildare, and in the nineteenth century it emerged as the favorite. It has always been the preferred form in this country. Gerald R. Ford, thirty-eighth president, was both the first vice-president and first president not popularly elected to either office.

## Gideon

Hebrew, "to hew, cut down." Var: **Gedeon, Gid.**

A judge and leader of Israel, whose victory over the invading Midianites is described in the Book of Judges. The name was brought to America by the Pilgrims, but it has never enjoyed great popularity. It is known primarily because of a group called the Gideons, who place copies of the Bible in hotel rooms.

## Gilbert

Old German, "bright pledge." Var: **Bert, Bertie, Berty, Gib, Gibb, Gibbs, Gil, Gilberto, Gill.**

A name that occurs in the tales of Robin Hood, it was familiar in England and France during the Middle Ages and continued in slight use until about the 1920s. It is seldom seen today. The early American painter Gilbert Stuart was celebrated for his portraits of George Washington.

## Glen

Scottish, "valley." Var: **Glenn, Glyn, Glynn.**

A Celtic name with variations in Irish and Welsh, it is commonly known because of a number of Scottish landmarks, especially the Great Glen of Scotland. Glenn Miller headed the most popular of all the big bands in the period before World War II; he disappeared during an army flight in 1944. Singer Glen Campbell.

## Grant

Old French, "great." Var: **Gran, Granny.**

This is a short form of English place names and first names like *Grantland* ("great plain") and *Grantley* ("great meadow"), but it is also a family name and first name in its own right, with roots in Scotland. Ulysses S. Grant, commander of the Union armies during the Civil War, was the eighteenth president. American parents used his last name rather than his first in naming boys, perhaps because it was easier to spell.

## Gregory

Greek, "watchman." Var: **Greg, Gregg, Gregor, Gregorio.**

Initially known because of two early saints, it became firmly established as a result of being selected by sixteen popes, more than any other name except *John*. Many are notable, including Gregory I of the sixth century, who revised church music (Gregorian chant or plainsong), and Gregory XIII, who introduced in 1582 the reformed calendar (Gregorian calendar) still in general use.

By the thirteenth century the name was familiar in Britain, often as *Gregour*, and many family names developed from it, among them the Scottish MacGregor ("son of Gregor"). Its popularity declined with the Puritans, and it was never a preferred name in America until the 1950s. Since then it has appeared more frequently, a trend for which actor Gregory Peck may be partly responsible.

— H —

### Harold

Old English, "army power." Var: **Hal, Harald, Harry, Herold.** See also **Henry, Walter.**

A favorite among royal families in Scandinavia, where the original meaning was slightly different ("strong warrior"). A tenth-century Harold was the first Christian king of Denmark, and three Danish kings, one named Harold, ruled England in the following century. The last Saxon king was also Harold, killed by the Norman invaders at Hastings in 1066. Since then no English king has had the name. It went out of fashion under Norman rule and was revived only in the 1800s. Toward the end of the century the form *Harry* became popular in the United States. Two famous Americans: singer Harry Lillis (Bing) Crosby and Harry S Truman, thirty-third president.

**Harvey**

Breton, "battle-worthy." Var: **Harv, Harve, Harvy, Hervey.**

St. Harvey was a sixth-century monk in Brittany, and the name was taken to England by the Normans. It endured mainly as a family name; the physician William Harvey described the circulation of the blood in the seventeenth century. Some two hundred years later it began to be used as a first name, and one recipient in the United States was Harvey Firestone, who founded the tire company. In 1945 Mary Chase received a Pulitzer Prize for a play of this name, later a movie with James Stewart, in which Harvey was a six-foot-tall white rabbit invisible to everyone but the principal character.

**Henry**

Old German, "ruler of the home." Var: **Enrico, Enrique, Hal, Hank, Harry, Heinrich, Hen, Hendrick, Hendrik, Henri, Henrik.** See also **Harold.**

When applied to British monarchs, the names *Henry* and *Edward* are tied at eight each; kings with the former name ruled, with some interruptions, from the twelfth to the sixteenth century. Originally German, the name arrived in England from France, and the English attempt to pronounce the French *Henri* gave rise to the form *Harry*. This was the customary version of the name in Britain until the 1600s; the short form was *Hal*.

By the time the English colonies were established in the New World, the pronunciation *Henry* was generally accepted, and the confusion between the two seldom arose in America. The most familiar short form in America became *Hank*, from the Dutch and German, and sometimes *Hen*. The name was very fashionable in the 1800s, but like many other names of that time it has declined in popularity. Actor Henry Fonda; Hank Aaron, member of the Baseball Hall of Fame and the leading home-run hitter (755) of all time.

## Herbert

Old German, "bright army." Var: **Bert, Bertie, Berty, Harbert, Hebert, Herb, Herbie.**

Another name that came to England with the Normans and developed into a family name. It was adopted again as a first name toward the end of the eighteenth century, remaining in fashion for more than one hundred years. Herbert Hoover, thirty-first president. The long-time political cartoonist Herbert L. Block is known as Herblock.

## Herman

Old German, "man of the army." Var: **Armand, Armando, Ermanno, Harman, Harmon, Herm, Hermann, Hermie.**

Familiar for over one thousand years in German-speaking countries, this name is relatively unusual in that its American popularity in the nineteenth and early twentieth centuries was never associated with naming patterns in England, where it has seldom been given. Two authors whose novels often deal with the sea: Herman Melville (*Moby Dick*) and Herman Wouk (*The Caine Mutiny*).

## Horace

Latin, "of Horatius." Var: **Horacio, Horatio.**

From a Roman clan name which may derive from *hora*, the Latin word for hour. Horace was one of the great Latin poets, and a revival of interest in the Greek and Latin classics made his name fashionable in sixteenth-century England. For about two hundred years the Italian form *Horatio* was predominant, followed by the

French *Horace*. In 1872 Horace Greeley was an unsuccessful Democratic candidate for president. As editor of the *New York Tribune*, he is credited with the famous advice, "Go West, young man!"

## Howard

Old English, "chief guardian." Var: **Howey, Howie.**

A family name from thirteenth-century England whose origin is uncertain; it seems to have been the title of a medieval official. Use as a first name began in the nineteenth century, and in the early 1900s it achieved wide popularity in this country. There are many examples: Senator Howard Baker; TV sportscaster Howard Cosell; novelist Howard Fast; aviator, industrialist, and financier Howard Hughes; and the pioneer of restaurant franchising, Howard Johnson.

## Hugh

Old German, "mind, thought." Var: **Hew, Huey, Hughie, Hugo, Ugo.**

A royal house of France was founded by Hugh Capet (Hugh in the Cape) and ruled from the tenth to the fourteenth century; later kings are considered by the French to be their descendants. When the name was brought to England by the Normans, it was originally *Hugo*. Like many other Norman names, it became established through branches of a family (as Hughes, Hewes, Hewett, etc.), but unlike most of the others it also kept its role as a first name, possibly because of a thirteenth-century bishop and saint named Hugh. Even so, it has remained an unusual first name in England and the United States.

— I —

## Ian

Hebrew, "God is gracious." Var: **Iain**.

See **John**. A Scottish form of the name, it was practically unknown in the United States until the 1960s but has grown steadily in popularity since then. Ian Fleming, creator of the James Bond novels.

## Ira

Hebrew, "watchful." Var: **Ire**.

Listed in the Old Testament as the name of an officer in King David's guard. It has been chosen in the United States on a small but steady basis for about one hundred years. Lyricist Ira Gershwin, brother of composer George Gershwin.

## Irving

Old English, "boar friend." Var: **Ervin, Erwin, Irv, Irvin, Irwin**.

The boar played an important role in medieval life. It was not only a creature to be pursued in periodic hunts but was a symbol of ferocity and strength. The name survived as a family name in England; *Irvin* and *Irwin* were first names added in the United States. Composer Irving Berlin.

## Isaac

Hebrew, "laughing one." Var: **Ike, Isaak, Izak, Izaak, Itzak**.

A son born to Sarah and Abraham late in their lives, he was the father of Esau and Jacob, according to the Book of Genesis. Three very different namesakes in the seventeenth century strengthened it as a first name: St. Isaac Jogues, a French missionary martyred in North America; Izaak Walton, author of *The Compleat Angler*, the first guide to fishing; and Isaac Newton, who first described the law of gravity.

## Ivan

Hebrew, "God is gracious." Var: **Yvan.**

See **John.** This is the Russian form which, like *Ian* and other versions, has been selected since the 1960s by some American parents in place of the traditional forms. Tennis star Ivan Lendl.

— J —

## Jack

Hebrew, "God is gracious." Var: **Jackie, Jacky, Jock, Jocko.**

See **John.** As a variation of the most familiar masculine name in English, it was already established by the fourteenth century as a general term for a man or a boy. The range of its applications gradually expanded to make it a name for a character in nursery rhymes ("Jack and Jill"), fairy tales ("Jack and the Beanstalk"), a representation of winter (Jack Frost), various birds and animals (jack rabbit), plants and trees (jack pine), toys (jack-in-the-box), prizes (jackpot), tools (jackknife), machines (jackhammer), occupations (lumberjack), and eventually someone handy at everything ("jack of all trades...") but expert at nothing ("... and master of none"). In many cases where jack is a common noun for a tool or instrument, it probably indicates that the device replaced human labor, as with a jack used for raising heavy objects.

A popular belief is that *Jack* must be related to *Jacques*, the French version of *James*, since it shares the form *Jackie* with the feminine *Jacqueline*. However, name researchers have found no record of *Jack* being used in place of either *Jacques* or *James*. It apparently stems from the Dutch and Flemish *Jan*, which became *Jankin* and then *Jackin*; in a similar fashion, the Scottish *Jock* evolved from *Jon*. Golf champion Jack Nicklaus; Jackie Robinson, the first black player in major league baseball; comedian Jackie Gleason.

## Jacob

Hebrew, "following after, supplanting." Var: **Jack, Jake, Jakie, Jakob.** See also **James.**

As told in Genesis, Jacob was the younger son of Isaac and Rebecca, brother of Esau and, ultimately, after his name was changed to Israel, the patriarch of the Hebrew nation. In a dream he was promised God's blessing and had a vision of a ladder connecting heaven and earth (Jacob's ladder), with angels rising and descending. Although the name was known in the Middle Ages, it was overshadowed by the related form *James*. When the Anglican or Authorized version of the Bible appeared in 1611, the latter name was given to the two apostles in the New Testament but *Jacob* was retained for the Old Testament patriarch. Subsequently, it was taken up by the Puritans and brought to the New World.

## James

Hebrew, "following after, supplanting." Var: **Diego,
Giacomo, Hamish, Jacques, Jaime, Jamey, Jamie,
Jayme, Jim, Jimmie, Jimmy, Seamus**. See also **Jacob**.

In the Middle Ages the name *Jacob* came to be ren-
dered in Latin in two different ways—as *Jacobus* and
*Jacomus*. The two gave rise to a number of versions that
initially were more or less interchangeable. For example, the French *Jacques*, derived from *Jacob*, became
identified with *James*; the reign of James I in early
seventeenth-century England is called the Jacobean rather
than the Jamesian period. In familiar use, however, *James*
emerged as the preferred form.

Two of the original twelve apostles are known as James
the Great and James the Less—possibly because the second was chosen by Jesus later or was simply smaller than
the other. According to legend, the first James preached
in Spain, and his body was taken there after his execution
in Jerusalem. His shrine at Santiago de Compostela in
northwestern Spain was one of the most famous in Europe
during the Middle Ages, and he became Spain's patron
saint. The capital of Chile and many other Latin American cities are named after him, as is the California city
of San Diego.

In Britain the popularity of *James* began in Scotland,
where it was the name of five kings of the Stuart line.
The sixth was crowned James I of England in 1603, and
he was the first to call himself the king of Great Britain.
As with *Charles*, however, the name has not been lucky
for British monarchs; the second and last James was
deposed in 1688. Conversely, it has been the most
frequent of all names among United States presidents.
There have been six called *James*, including the fourth
(Madison), fifth (Monroe), eleventh (Polk), fifteenth

(Buchanan), twentieth (Garfield), and thirty-ninth (Carter).

The name still ranks high on most top-ten lists. Familiar forms are *Jim* and *Jimmy*, but the Scottish *Jamie* is now given mainly as a girl's name in this country.

## Jason

Greek, "healer." Var: **Jase, Jay.**

In Greek mythology, Jason was an exiled prince raised by a centaur after Pelias, his half-brother, seized his throne. With the hope that Jason would be killed, Pelias sent him in search of the Golden Fleece, which possessed magical powers and was guarded by an enormous serpent. He set out in the ship *Argo* with his companions, called the Argonauts; after many adventures his expedition was successful. The name also appears in the New Testament designating a relative of Paul the Apostle. It may possibly be a Greek variation of the Hebrew *Joshua*.

Neither of these references seems to have had any connection with *Jason*'s sudden rise to prominence around the end of the 1960s, which apparently was sparked by the popularity of characters in TV dramas. Actor Jason Robards, Jr., won an Academy Award for his role in *All the President's Men* (1976).

## Jeffrey

Old German, "God's peace" or "country peace." Var: **Jeff, Jeffery, Jeffry, Jeffy.** See also **Geoffrey.**

The name was often confused with *Godfrey* during the Middle Ages, which accounts for the two slightly different definitions. Although the "G" form is preferred in England, *Jeffrey* was an old written variant and explains the spelling of family names like Jeffries. It was sometimes given in nineteenth-century America in tribute to

Thomas Jefferson, as in the name of the president of the
Confederacy, Jefferson Davis; however, it was never used
widely until the middle of this century, when it began to
climb rapidly on the popularity charts. Novelist Jeffrey
Archer.

## Jeremy

Hebrew, "exalted by God." Var: **Jere, Jerry.**

Jeremiah, the famous Hebrew prophet who warned of
the coming defeat and captivity of Israel by the Baby-
lonians, was also called Jeremias and Jeremy in the New
Testament. The latter version was in general use by the
1300s, and it has always been the most familiar form in
England, even though the Old Testament name was revived by the Puritans. Like *Jeffrey*, it fell from fashion
in the United States in the late nineteenth century but has
had a strong recent recovery. Actor Jeremy Irons.

## Jerome

Greek, "holy name." Var: **Gerome, Jerrome, Jerry.**

St. Jerome was the Christian scholar responsible for
the Latin Vulgate (popular) translation of the Bible at the
end of the fourth century. In the medieval era the name
was familiar in a variety of forms, including the Italian
*Geronimo* and the Spanish *Jeronimo* (pronounced and
sometimes spelled *Hieronimo*). The latter is the name of
a principal character in Kyd's *Spanish Tragedy* (1594),
the first great revenge thriller of the English theater.

Nearly three centuries later the same version of the
name came to American attention in an odd way. It was
taken by the leader of an Indian uprising of the 1880s,
one of the last in United States history. The settlers in
the Southwest pronounced it with a "G" and called him
Geronimo, thus unwittingly giving the Apache chieftain

an Italian name. Author J. D. (Jerome David) Salinger
(*The Catcher in the Rye*).

## Jesse

Hebrew, "wealthy." Var: **Jess, Jessie.**

Another possible definition is "God exists." The biblical Jesse lived in Bethlehem and was the father of King David. Seldom used in England before the Protestant Reformation of the sixteenth century, the name was adopted by the Puritans but was never a particular favorite. Since the 1960s it has benefited from the renewal of interest in Old Testament names. Political and religious leader Jesse Jackson.

## Jody

Hebrew, "addition" or "God adds." Var: **Jodey.** See also the feminine **Jodie.**

Unlike most names used for both girls and boys, this one has a different origin in each case. As a feminine name, it is a variation of *Judith* that also stands by itself. As a name for boys, it is a short form of *Joseph* found mainly in the South. Journalist and TV commentator Jody Powell, former press secretary in the Carter White House.

## Joel

Hebrew, "Jehovah is God." Var: **Joley.**

The same basic elements that make up *Elijah* are used here in reverse order. It is another Old Testament name whose common use began only after the Reformation. Joel was a prophet who foretold the day of judgment, but the name also appears in at least ten other biblical references.

## John

Hebrew, "God is gracious." Var: **Giovanni, Hans, Jan, Janos, Jean, Johann, Johannes, Johnnie, Johnny, Jon, Juan, Zane.** See also **Evan, Ian, Ivan, Jack, Jonathan, Sean.**

Two major New Testament figures had this name: John the Baptist, the famous preacher executed by King Herod, and John the Apostle, author of the fourth Gospel and possibly the Book of Revelation. Brought back from the East by crusaders, the name began to spread in Europe about the twelfth century and was soon a favorite. Its standing in England was not influenced by royal sponsorship, for there was only one King John, who was unpopular with his people and forced to sign the document known as Magna Carta in 1215. However, it has been the name of some of the leading English poets, including John Donne, John Milton, and John Keats.

In this country it ranks second only to *James* as a name for presidents. The second and sixth presidents, John Adams and John Quincy Adams, were father and son. John Tyler, the tenth, was the first vice-president to succeed to the office after a president's death (William Henry Harrison). The thirty-fifth president was John F. Kennedy.

## Jonah

Hebrew, "dove." Var: **Jona, Jonas.**

The Old Testament prophet always remembered as the one swallowed by a great fish (the Bible does not mention a whale); three days later he emerged unharmed. Another name revived by the Puritans, it has shown new strength since the 1970s.

## Jonathan

Hebrew, "gift of God." Var: **Jonathon.** See also **John.**

A name that occurs often in the Old Testament, most notably referring to a son of King Saul and close friend of David. It has the same meaning as *Nathaniel*, although a different Hebrew word for God is used. It has always taken second place to the more popular *John*, but recently it has gained popularity.

## Joseph

Hebrew, "addition" or "God adds." Var: **Giuseppe, Jo, Joe, Joey, Jose, Jozef.** See also **Jody.**

The history of this name is unusual in that it has followed two separate paths to popularity. For many centuries it was given in honor of the Joseph whose eventful life is recounted in the Book of Genesis. Son of Jacob and Rachel, he was sold into slavery in Egypt at the age of seventeen by his envious brothers; only a dozen years later he was the governor of Egypt and the advisor to the pharaoh. The name took on new life in England after the Protestant Reformation.

However, at about the same time, in the seventeenth century, there was a growing devotion in Catholic countries to Joseph of Nazareth, husband of Mary. Advised in a dream about the impending birth, he took Mary with him to his ancestral town of Bethlehem to enroll in the Roman census, and there the child was born in a stable. After a period of exile in Egypt to escape the anger of King Herod, Joseph returned to Nazareth with Mary and Jesus to continue his work as a carpenter. There was a family visit to Jerusalem when Jesus was twelve, but little more is heard of Joseph after that time.

These two historical strands combined in the nineteenth century to give the name special popularity in the

United States. And yet, curiously, it has never been the name of a president or vice-president. In this century, it has been known primarily among sports figures, from baseball star Joe DiMaggio to football quarterbacks Joe Namath and Joe Montana.

### Joshua

Hebrew, "God is salvation." Var: **Josh.**

A Hebrew slave in Egypt, he was one of the early followers of Moses and succeeded him as head of Israel; the promised land was reached under his leadership. (*Jesus* may also be derived from the same root.) The name has been steadily but not widely chosen since the Protestant Reformation. It recently was taken up again by parents in the revival of Old Testament names.

### Julian

Latin, "downy hair." Var: **Giuliano, Giulio, Jule, Jules, Julie, Julio, Julius.**

From the Latin clan name made famous by Julius Caesar. Strictly speaking, it means "of or belonging to Julius," from the Latin *Julianus*, but *Julian* is the version that became more popular in the Middle Ages than the original. Pioneer science fiction writer Jules Verne.

# — K —

### Keith

Scottish, "wood." Var: **Keithe.**

The term also conveys the wider meaning of "a wooded area." A place name that became a family name and then,

in the nineteenth century, a Scottish first name. It entered
more general use about fifty years ago. Guitarist Keith
Richards of the Rolling Stones.

## Kenneth

Scottish, "handsome." Var: **Ken, Kennie, Kenny.**
This old Gaelic name has roots in both Scotland and
Ireland, where it was the name of an early Irish saint.
But it was a ninth-century king of Scotland who made it
well known, and for most of its history it has been most
strongly associated with families of Scottish origin. It
was a preferred name in America from the period before
World War II until the 1960s, but its popularity has been
in decline since then. Football star Ken Anderson.

## Kent

Old English, "border or coastal area." Var: **Ken, Kennie, Kenny.**
A county in southeastern England. The name may also
be related to Celtic words for "chief" and "bright." It
began to appear as a first name early in this century.

## Kevin

Irish, "handsome at birth." Var: **Kev, Kevan.**
This represents a slight variation of the original Gaelic
word for *Kenneth*. The name has long been a favorite
among Irish families, aided in this century by a popular
ballad, "Kevin Barry." It has benefited from the more
recent revival of Irish names. Actor Kevin McCarthy.

## Kimball

Welsh, "warrior chief." Var: **Kim, Kimbell, Kimmie.**
See also the feminine **Kimberly.**

A family name that has also been linked to an Old English word with a similar meaning, "bold leader." It gained attention as a first name after the publication of Rudyard Kipling's popular novel *Kim* (1901). Used for several decades as a first name and nickname for boys, especially in England, it has almost disappeared with the rapid rise of *Kim* as a girl's name since the 1950s.

— L —

### Lance

Old German, "land." Var: **Lancelin, Lancelot, Launcelot.**

Two common assumptions about this thirteenth-century name are that it is derived from the medieval weapon and that the longer form *Lancelot* is the original version. Actually, *Lance* is probably the earlier form, and it has been traced to the Old German word for land. In the Arthurian legend, Sir Lancelot was one of the Knights of the Round Table.

### Lawrence

Latin, "from Laurentium." Var: **Larrie, Larry, Lars, Laurance, Laurence, Laurent, Laurie, Lauritz, Loren, Lorenz, Lorenzo, Lorin, Lorne, Lorrie, Lorry.**

Initially, it was a term designating someone from a Roman town named for the laurel or bay tree; the laurel wreath was awarded as a symbol of victory or great achievement. Many American cities are also named for the tree, but similar geographical names, such as the Laurentian Mountains in Canada and the St. Lawrence

River, are named for a third-century martyr in Rome who was a favorite saint in the Middle Ages.

Appropriately, the name has been kept in fashion at different periods of history by the reputation or accomplishment of an individual bearer. Archbishop Laurence O'Toole of Dublin was a popular figure of the twelfth century. In fifteenth-century Italy, Lorenzo de Medici was the ruler of Tuscany and patron of the arts in Florence. Laurence Sterne, author of *Tristram Shandy* (1760), was a pioneer of the English novel. It was the family name of the best-known Lawrence of this century: Thomas E. Lawrence ("Lawrence of Arabia"). A film based on his World War I exploits won the Academy Award in 1962. Actor Sir Laurence Olivier.

## Lee

Old English, "meadow." Var: see the feminine **Leigh.**
There has been some intermingling of the two forms, but *Lee* is the spelling generally used for boys. In the South it may be given to commemorate Confederate General Robert E. Lee. Golf champion Lee Trevino.

## Leo

Latin, "lion." Var: **Lee, Leon.**
The long history of this name is demonstrated by the fact that it has been taken by thirteen popes. They extend from the fifth-century Leo I, who is supposed to have personally persuaded Attila the Hun to refrain from attacking Rome, to Leo XIII in the late nineteenth century. Leo Tolstoy, author of *War and Peace* (1866).

## Leonard

Old German, "lion courage." Var: **Len, Lenard, Lennard, Lennie, Lenny, Leonardo.**

A medieval saint's name that has had steady if not strong support for many centuries. The most famous bearer of the past five hundred years is still Leonardo da Vinci, Renaissance scientist, engineer, inventor, and painter of "The Last Supper" and what is popularly known as the "Mona Lisa."

## Leslie

Old English, "small meadow." Var: **Les, Lesly.** See also the feminine **Lesley.**

Although its use for boys has continued in England, this place name and family name has increasingly been preferred for girls in the United States.

## Lloyd

Welsh, "gray." Var: **Loy, Loyde.** See also **Floyd.**

The well-known Lloyd's of London, formed originally in the seventeenth century to provide insurance for shipping, took its name from a coffeehouse where shipowners, merchants, and brokers met to do business. Actor Lloyd Bridges.

## Louis

Old German, "famous warrior." Var: **Aloysius, Lew, Lewis, Lou, Ludovic, Ludwig, Luigi, Luis.**

Despite its Germanic origin, this is the most familiar of all French names. Rulers of France named *Louis* have included one emperor, Louis Napoleon Bonaparte (who called himself Napoleon III), and eighteen kings. One of them, the son of the executed Louis XVI and Marie Antoinette, died in prison and never took the throne. The last French king was Louis-Philippe, who ruled briefly in 1830.

Until this century, *Lewis* was the more familiar form

in England as a family name and first name, but usage
now seems to follow the traditional American preference
for *Louis*. The importance of French influence in the New
World was represented by the enormous Louisiana Territory, purchased by the United States from France in
1803 for about $15 million. The city of St. Louis, which
became the point of departure for pioneers heading west,
was named after Louis IX, crusader-king of the thirteenth
century.

The popularity of the name reached a peak in the early
1900s; although no longer in the preferred group, it has
never dropped completely from use. Musician Louis
Armstrong.

## Luke

Greek, "from Lucania." Var: **Luca, Lucas, Lucian,
Lucien, Lucio, Lucius, Lukas.**

This one syllable combines three separate names—
the Greek name given above, the similar *Lucian*, whose
meaning is uncertain, and the Latin *Lucius* ("light"). Until
the late nineteenth century, they retained separate iden-
tities, but *Luke* has generally replaced them in the United
States. Its popularity still lags rather far behind that of
the names of the three other New Testament evangelists,
Matthew, Mark, and John. Luke, author of the third Gospel and companion of the apostle Paul, was reputed to
be a physician.

# — M —

## Malcolm

Scottish, "servant or disciple of Columba." Var: **Mal,
Malc.**

St. Columba was a sixth-century missionary from Ireland to Scotland who is credited with having established over one hundred monasteries. This name described his followers and converts. It was later the name of four Scottish kings, including the Malcolm who, as dramatized in Shakespeare's *Macbeth*, regained his kingdom in 1057. The name was rare outside Scotland until the early 1900s, but it is occasionally seen in the United States. Actor Malcolm McDowell.

## Mark

Latin, "martial." Var: **Marc, Marco, Marcos, Marcus.** See also **Anthony, Martin.**

From a Roman clan name (*Marcius*) and first name (*Marcus*) that are both believed to be related to Mars, the god of war. A similar form is *Marcellus*, or "little Mark," which gives names such as the French *Marcel* and the Italian *Marcello*.

The second Gospel was written by Mark, who apparently had many of the firsthand details from Peter, the leader of the twelve apostles. Mark is said to have traveled to Italy, and the name has always been popular there, especially in Venice, where the famous church of St. Mark is located. In the thirteenth century, the Venetian Marco Polo visited the court of Kublai Khan and brought back the first accurate description of China. The name was introduced in England about the same time, but it was seldom used until the 1800s, when it was adopted in Britain and the United States. However, the widely known American author Mark Twain (Samuel Clemens) took his pen name not from *Mark* but from an expression used by Mississippi riverboat pilots.

It dropped from fashion early in this century, and then, in the 1960s, it began a strong revival. Football star Marcus Allen.

## Martin

Latin, "of Mars." Var: **Mart, Marten, Martino, Marty, Martyn.**

Mars was the Roman god of war (and also of agriculture); both the planet closest to the Earth and the month of March are named for him. The transfer of the name from Roman to Christian tradition is symbolized by the first St. Martin, a soldier in the fourth century who left the army to become a monk and eventually the bishop of Tours in France. His dedication to the poor made his name popular during the Middle Ages. Unlike the names of many other saints, it continued in favor after the Protestant Reformation because of the reputation of Martin Luther.

## Matthew

Hebrew, "gift of God." Var: **Matt, Matteo, Matthias, Matthieu, Mattie, Matty.**

Like *Jonathan* and *Nathaniel*, this name is a reworking of essentially the same name elements. Matthew, author of the first Gospel, was a publican, or tax collector, meaning that he was a servant of the Roman government in Palestine. By inviting him to join the band of disciples, Jesus indicated that even those disapproved of by others were welcome to follow him. The Greek form of the name, Matthias, was given to the disciple who replaced Judas Iscariot.

For most of its history, *Matthew* has been a steady though unspectacular favorite, especially in the nineteenth century. Matthew Arnold was a leading English poet and critic, and United States naval officer Matthew Perry opened Japan to American trade. Since the early 1970s, however, preference for the name has increased dramatically, and it is now on most top-ten lists.

## Melvin

Scottish, "chief." Var: **Malvin, Mel, Melvyn.**

A number of other origins are suggested; it may also be a place name. In the United States it has been particularly associated with baseball: Mel Ott, Hall of Fame member from the former New York Giants; Mel Allen, long-time voice of the New York Yankees.

## Michael

Hebrew, "who is like God?" Var: **Michal, Michail, Michel, Mick, Mickey, Mickie, Miguel, Mike, Mikey, Mischa, Mitch, Mitchell.**

Never really out of fashion since the thirteenth century, the name had a new burst of popularity in the 1960s and has remained a leading favorite in all English-speaking countries. The feminine *Michelle* is equally popular.

With Gabriel, Michael is one of the only two angels mentioned by name in both the Old and New Testaments. But where Gabriel is portrayed as a bearer of glad tidings, Michael is shown as the guardian and champion of humans, leading the fight against Satan. To emphasize that a child was being named for this Michael, the practice of adding "angel" to the name began in Italy during the Middle Ages. It was given to the most famous of all Renaissance artists, Michelangelo Buonarroti, sculptor, architect, poet, and painter of the Sistine Chapel.

## Milton

Old English, "mill town." Var: **Milt, Miltie, Milty.**

A medieval place name that became a family name. Its use as a first name was probably influenced most of all by the English poet John Milton of the seventeenth century. Familiar in the United States in the early 1900s, it gained prominence thanks to "Mr. Television," Milton Berle.

## Moses

Hebrew, "drawn out." Var: **Moe, Moise, Moishe, Mose, Moshe, Moss, Moyse.**

Like his brother Aaron, Moses was born during the Hebrew bondage in Egypt, and his name may also be related to an Egyptian word meaning "born." Although the two brothers led the Israelites out of captivity, they were prohibited by God from entering the promised land because of disobedience; however, Moses was able to view it before his death. The name was occasionally given outside Jewish families in the Middle Ages, but the Puritans introduced it into more general use. Basketball star Moses Malone; playwright Moss Hart.

## Murray

Scottish, "seabound." Var: **Murrey, Murry.**

A place name and clan name in Scotland, it is sometimes given as a first name. In the United States it may also be used as a variant of *Maurice* or *Morris* ("Moor").

## — N —

## Nathaniel

Hebrew, "gift of God." Var: **Nat, Nate, Nathan, Nathanael.**

The name *Nathan* means "gift" in Hebrew. The Old Testament Nathan was a prophet who reproached King David for arranging the death of Uriah so that he could marry Bathsheba, Uriah's wife. In the New Testament,

Nathanael appears only in the Gospel of John; he is believed to be the same apostle called Bartholomew in the first three Gospels. Combined with different elements for God, *Nathan* also forms part of *Jonathan* and *Matthew*.

Both *Nathan* and *Nathaniel* were introduced in America by the Puritans. Nathan Hale was an early hero of the Revolutionary War; Nathaniel Hawthorne wrote *The Scarlet Letter* (1850) and other novels and stories; Nat "King" Cole was one of the most popular singers of the mid-twentieth century.

## Neil

Irish, "champion." Var: **Neal, Neale, Neill, Nial, Niel, Niles, Nils.**

Another possible definition is "brave." Apparently, the name originated at about the fifth century in Ireland, where it was the basis for the family name O'Neill. A similar name arrived in England six centuries later with the Normans and was incorrectly written in Latin as *Nigellus*; this gave the first name *Nigel*, a favorite in Scotland. The earlier version continued as a family name, including such forms as Nielson and Nelson. The latter was taken as a first name in honor of Horatio Nelson, who led the British fleet that defeated the French and Spanish at Trafalgar in 1805. Toward the end of the nineteenth century, *Neil* itself returned as a first name.

It became a favorite in the United States in the 1960s. The name is also sometimes given to girls as *Neal* or *Neale*. Neil Armstrong, first man on the moon (1969).

## Nicholas

Greek, "victory of the people." Var: **Cole, Klaus, Niccolo, Nick, Nickie, Nicky, Nicol, Nicolai, Nicolas, Niki, Nikita, Nikolas.**

One of the most popular saints of the Middle Ages, Nicholas of Myra was the bishop of a region in Turkey early in the fourth century. Among other things, he is the patron of Greece and the former patron of Russia, but most of the stories connected with his name firmly established him as the patron of children. In medieval Germany and Holland, someone dressed as a bishop distributed small gifts to children on the eve of his feast day (December 6). When this custom was introduced in England and America, the date was transferred to Christmas, and St. Nicholas became Santa Claus.

## Noah

Hebrew, "repose." Var: **Noe.**

As told in Genesis, the story of Noah and the ark is one of the most familiar in the Bible. Noah not only was chosen by God to survive the great flood but was given precise directions as to the ark's construction; its provisions and passengers were also described in detail. After the flood, it was Noah's responsibility to make a new beginning. The name was adopted by the Puritans and was fairly common in America until the late nineteenth century. Noah Webster not only compiled the first American dictionary (1828) but also published widely used texts and spelling books for schoolchildren.

## Norman

Old English, "man from the north." Var: **Norm, Normie, Normy.**

It would seem likely that this name would stem from the Norman Conquest, but its presence in England preceded the invasion. It was applied generally to any intruders or settlers from the north; the Normans of the eleventh century were more specifically the Norman

French. It died out as a first name in England by the fifteenth century but lived on in Scotland, and by the 1800s it was considered almost exclusively Scottish. It became fashionable in America early in this century, then declined in the 1960s. Author Norman Mailer.

## — O —

### Oliver

Old German, "elf counsel," and Old French, "olive tree." Var: **Olivero, Olivier, Ol, Ollie, Olly.**

Unlike the feminine version of the name, which derived directly from the olive tree, the masculine form followed a more roundabout path. It was apparently the German version of a Scandinavian word that ultimately became the first name *Olaf*; this in turn was influenced by the Norman word for the tree, so that it reached England as *Oliver*. It was popular until the seventeenth century, taking on new strength with the rule of Oliver Cromwell, but it fell suddenly from favor when the monarchy was restored in 1660. By the nineteenth century, as shown by Dickens' *Oliver Twist*, it was considered an appropriate name for a poor orphan.

No similar tradition prevailed in New England, where the name retained its popularity until the early 1900s. Oliver Wendell Holmes was a famous Boston physician and author, and his son of the same name was a justice of the United States Supreme Court. It made a slight comeback beginning in the 1970s.

### Owen

Greek, "of noble birth." Var: **Owin.**

See **Eugene.** This is the Welsh form of the name,

whose origin is sometimes confused with *Evan*, a Welsh version of *John*. The second film (1930) made from Owen Wister's *The Virginian* set the style for many Hollywood Westerns.

— P —

## Patrick

Latin, "of nobility." Var: **Paddy, Padraic, Padraig, Pat, Patric, Patrice, Patricio, Patrizio.**

The patrician class originally consisted of the noble families of the Roman republic; by extension, the term came to mean anyone of noble birth or quality. As a first name, *Patrick* was in early use outside Rome; the missionary to Ireland was born around 380, probably in Scotland. According to legend, he was captured in his youth by pirates and sold into slavery, but he escaped to France and studied in a monastery. The rest of his life was spent as a missionary among the Irish, although he may have visited Scotland and England. There are many stories associated with his name, the most famous being that he cleared his adopted country of serpents. He is the best-known patron saint of Ireland, but there are two others, Bridget and Columba.

## Paul

Latin, "small." Var: **Pablo, Paolo, Paulie, Paulo, Pavel.**

Paul the Apostle, one of the founders of the Christian religion, studied in Jerusalem as a young man and seemed destined to become a leading Hebrew scholar. But on a journey from Jerusalem to Damascus, he was converted

to Christianity after having a vision that left him blind
for three days. From that time on he traveled tirelessly
around the Mediterranean, establishing churches, preach-
ing and interpreting God's message, and enduring many
physical hardships. Often imprisoned, he was martyred
in Rome during the persecution of the Christians by the
Emperor Nero in A.D. 67 or 68.

Although his name was widely known, it did not come
into general use for many centuries. Possibly the reason
was that it customarily took second place to that of St.
Peter when the two were linked; they even share a common feast day (June 29). After the Protestant Reformation, when *Peter* was associated with Rome and the
papacy, *Paul* began to grow steadily in popularity, and
it has continued to be a preferred name among many
generations of parents.

Paul Revere, a silversmith, made a famous ride in
1775 to warn residents of Massachusetts of the British
advance. Actor Paul Newman; composer and singer Paul
McCartney; Pablo Picasso, one of the leading painters
of the twentieth century.

## Peter

Greek, "stone, rock." Var: **Pedro, Perry, Pete, Petey,
Pierce, Pierre, Piers, Piet, Pietr, Pietro.**

As described in the New Testament, Jesus gave this
name to the fisherman Simon as a symbol of the stead-
fastness of his faith. Peter became the leader of the twelve
apostles, the first bishop of Rome, and a martyr with St.
Paul during Nero's persecution of the Christians. The
church of St. Peter in Rome is built over his tomb.

In England, the name was familiar during the Middle
Ages, most frequently in the form *Piers*, but it went into
a sharp decline after Henry VIII broke with the pope in

1534. For nearly three centuries, literary references to it usually involved simple or rural characters. It returned to favor in the early 1900s, perhaps due in part to the continuing success of James M. Barrie's 1904 play, later a musical, *Peter Pan*. Actor Peter O'Toole; baseball star Pete Rose; singer Perry Como.

## Philip

Greek, "lover of horses." Var: **Felipe, Filippo, Phil, Phillip, Phillipe.**

Like *Peter*, this was the name of another in the original group of twelve apostles, but little more is known of him. In the ancient world the name was made famous by Philip of Macedonia, the father of Alexander the Great, and it was long a favorite with royalty. It was the name of six kings of France and five kings of Spain, including the monarch (Philip II) who launched the Armada against England; the Philippine Islands are named after the same king. His unpopularity in Britain caused the name to go out of fashion, and it wasn't revived there until the nineteenth century. Although never in the top rank of preferred names, it has remained in use ever since. Prince Philip is the husband of Queen Elizabeth II.

## — Q —

## Quentin

Latin, "fifth." Var: **Quent, Quint, Quintin.**

Related to a Roman clan name, it was also a personal name (*Quintus*) given to a fifth son; a similar use was made of *Septimus* and *Octavius* for seventh and eighth sons. Later on these names were given without regard to the order of birth. *Quentin*, the most familiar, reached England with the Normans in the eleventh century and lasted until about the fourteenth century, but it continued in favor in Scotland through the early 1700s. It received more general attention again with the publication of Sir Walter Scott's historical novel *Quentin Durward* (1823).

## Quincy

Old French, "fifth estate." Var: **Quince.**

Apparently, it is derived from a place name, which may have been French in origin, that became a family name, as with the nineteenth-century English author Thomas De Quincey. Composer Quincy Jones.

## Quinn

Irish, "wise." Var: **Quin, Quinlan.**

There is always the likelihood that names with this element are related in some way to "fifth," but some researchers suggest that *Quinn* comes from a Gaelic word with the meaning given above. It is the basis of a number of Irish family names.

# — R —

## Ralph

Scandinavian, "wolf counsel." Var: **Rafe, Rafer, Ralf, Raoul, Raul**

An old name found in England early in the Middle Ages. It was pronounced *Rafe*, rhyming with "safe," until recent times, even though the accepted spelling had become *Ralph* by the 1600s. The latter pronunciation was adopted in America. A similar Norman name, *Rolf* ("wolf fame"), eventually lost out to *Ralph*, but it turned into *Rollo* in France and *Rudolph* in Germany. Ralph Waldo Emerson was a famous philosopher and writer of the nineteenth century. Consumer activist Ralph Nader.

## Randolph

Old English,"wolf shield." Var: **Randal, Randall, Randolf, Randy.**

This was the medieval form of a first name that later became more popular as *Randal*; the original survived as a family name, and the Randolphs of Virginia played an important role in early American history. Edmund Randolph was both secretary of state and attorney general in George Washington's Cabinet. It was revived as a first name in the nineteenth century.

## Raphael

Hebrew, "God heals." Var: **Rafael, Rafaelle, Raffaelo, Rafe.**

With Gabriel and Michael, Raphael is the third angel mentioned by name in biblical writings; his story appears in the Book of Tobit. However, this book forms part of the Apocrypha, works whose authenticity was disputed by Hebrew scholars and that were excluded from the Old Testament. The same view was upheld by Protestant reformers of the sixteenth century. Thus the name was given mainly in Catholic countries, though it is seldom found today. Raffaelo Sanzio, called Raphael, was one of the great artists of Renaissance Italy.

## Raymond

Old German, "wise protection." Var: **Raimondo, Ramon, Ray, Raymound, Redmond.**

The "wise" element has also been defined as "counsel" or "advise." Brought to England by the Normans, the name was a favorite in the later Middle Ages because of two thirteenth-century saints, whose fame kept it alive especially in their native Spain. Elsewhere it lost preference until it was revived in the late 1800s, and it reached a peak in the United States in the 1930s. Raymond Chandler was one of the creators of the "private eye" mystery novel. Singer and musician Ray Charles.

## Reginald

Old English, "powerful force." Var: **Reg, Reggie, Reinald, Reinhold, Renault, Rinaldo.** See also **Rex, Ronald.**

A Norman name that took several forms in England, the most popular of which became the family name Reynolds. For several centuries *Reynold* was also the common pronunciation of the first name, but by the 1500s it was *Reginald* in both speech and spelling. Like many Norman names, it went out of fashion in the Elizabethan era but returned to favor in the nineteenth century. Baseball star Reggie Jackson.

## Rex

Latin, "king." Var: **Rexie.**

Although this name was in use prior to the 1900s, there seems to be no record of it as a separate or baptismal name until the present century. The assumption is that it was used as a short form of *Reginald*, like *Reg*. It has never been a familiar name in the United States. Actor Rex Harrison.

## Richard

Old German, "strong ruler." Var: **Dick, Dickie, Dicky, Ricardo, Rich, Richie, Rick, Rickie, Ricky, Rico, Ritchie.**

This is another name that reached England with the Normans. It gained great attention because of the exploits of the crusader-king Richard I (Richard the Lion-Hearted), but it suffered with the reputations of the next two Richards, especially the fifteenth-century Richard III, the last king to bear the name. While it was still given occasionally—an example is playwright Richard Sheridan, author of the classic comedy *The School for Scandal* (1777)—it didn't enter general use again until the Victorian period. Admiral Richard Byrd, explorer of the North and South Poles, was an American hero of the 1920s. Richard M. Nixon was the thirty-seventh United States president and the only one to resign the office. Olympic swimming champion Rick Carey; comedian Rich Little.

## Robert

Old German, "bright fame." Var: **Bob, Bobbie, Bobby, Rab, Rob, Robbie, Robby, Roberto, Robin, Rupert.**

This was one of the most popular Norman names, and it soon gave rise in England to a long list of rhyming nicknames (*Dob, Hob, Lob*), few of which are used now. It was a particular favorite in Scotland, where it was the name of three fourteenth-century kings, among them the national hero, Robert Bruce. Another hero was Rob Roy (now a drink), whose real name was Robert MacGregor, an eighteenth-century outlaw sometimes called the Robin Hood of Scotland (see **Roy**). As for Robin Hood himself, his legend had begun six centuries earlier; most historians agree that his adventures are probably based on folk stories rather than fact. It has been suggested that around his name coalesced many different tales of English resistance to Norman rule.

Some forms of *Robert* have become staples of English speech, as with a "bob" for a shilling, though no one knows exactly how it originated. The term "bobby" for a police officer is derived from the organization of the metropolitan police force under Sir Robert Peel in 1828. The name was also given to the familiar robin, a different bird in Europe from the one in America. Seldom out of fashion for two hundred years in the United States, *Robert* appeared in the 1980s on most top-ten lists. Poet Robert Frost was a four-time winner of the Pulitzer Prize. Novelist Robert Ludlum; comedian Bob Hope.

## Roderick

Old German, "famous rule." Var: **Rod, Roddie, Roddy, Roderic, Roderigo, Rodrigo, Rory.** See also **Broderick.**

Another Norman name that found a special welcome in Scotland, possibly because there was already a similar Scottish name meaning "red." Before the Norman invasion of Britain, it had already taken root in Spain as *Roderigo* (or *Ruy*), the name of the eleventh-century Spanish hero known as El Cid. It appeared in the title of an early English novel by Tobias Smollett, *The Adventures of Roderick Random* (1748). It also shares some short forms with *Rodney*, an Old English place name and family name with a different root ("reed island"). Actor Roddy McDowell; hockey star Rod Langway.

## Roger

Old German, "famous spear." Var: **Rodge, Rodger, Rogerio, Rogers, Ruggiero, Rutger.**

A name that was widely given in England during the Middle Ages, *Roger* suffered in the sixteenth century the same fate as a number of other preferred medieval names: it was associated with a typical country dweller or peasant. In turn, this association may have led to the very different meaning of "rogue," a word applied to vagrants and vagabonds uprooted from English rural areas. The origin of the pirate flag called the Jolly Roger is uncertain, but one possibility is that it designated a crew of rogues. The name was revived at the end of the nineteenth century. TV anchorman Roger Mudd.

## Ronald

Old English, "powerful force." Var: **Ron, Ronnie, Ronny.**

See **Reginald**, of which this is the Scottish form. It is a version that has become generally familiar, but another spelling, *Ranald*, is limited to Scotland. The name of the fortieth president, Ronald Reagan; baseball star Ron Guidry.

## Roy

Scottish, "red." Var: **Roye.**

The French word *roi* means "king," and the name is often given as a short form of names directly related to king, such as *Elroy*, *Leroy*, and *Royal*. Thus it's natural to assume that *Roy* itself has the same association. In terms of its history in Britain, however, the name comes from the Gaelic word for red. An illustration is offered by the eighteenth-century outlaw Rob Roy (see **Robert**), whose nickname meant "Robert the Red," taken from his red hair. Western entertainer Roy Rogers.

## Russell

Old French, "red." Var: **Russ, Rustie, Rusty.**

Like *Roy*, this is another name based on the color, but with a Norman French rather than a Scottish root. A well-established English family name, it was only adopted as a first name in the nineteenth century. Author and columnist Russell Baker.

## Ryan

Irish, "red." Var: **Rian.**

An Irish family name that was transformed in the 1970s, almost overnight, into one of the most popular first names in the United States. Some have credited the actor Ryan O'Neal, especially because of the highly successful film *Love Story* (1970), but it is also a name used for characters in various TV dramatic series. As with the Scottish *Roy*, this is a color name that is sometimes confused with the French word for king.

## ___ S ___

## Samuel

Hebrew, "heard by God." Var: **Sam, Sammie, Sammy.**

Another possible meaning is "name of God," but since Hannah, Samuel's mother, had prayed for so long to be blessed with a child, the definition given above seems more appropriate. Two books of the Old Testament bear his name, the first of which describes his key role in establishing the foundation of the kingdom of Israel. It was Samuel, judge and prophet, who anointed Saul as the first king, and later, when Saul went astray, it was Samuel who prepared David as his successor.

The name was unusual in Britain until the Protestant Reformation, but then it quickly became a favorite, associated with many authors and poets. Still the best known is probably Dr. Samuel Johnson, compiler of a dictionary of English (1755) and subject of James Boswell's *Life of Samuel Johnson*, generally considered the greatest biography in the language. The name also plays a role in American history, beginning with Samuel de Champlain, the seventeenth-century French explorer who discovered the lake that bears his name. Samuel Morse, regarded in the 1800s primarily as an artist, is remembered today as the inventor of Morse code. Above all, the name is known for Uncle Sam, the personification of our country, said to have originated during the War of 1812 because of the initials U.S. stamped on army supplies.

### Saul

Hebrew, "asked for." Var: **Sol, Solly, Zolly.**

An important name in biblical tradition. In the Old Testament, Saul was the first monarch of Israel, marking the transition from the rule of judges to the rule of kings; he was followed by a much more imposing figure, King David. The Apostle Paul in the New Testament was called at first Saul of Tarsus, from his birthplace in the southern part of Turkey on the Mediterranean. Unlike many other biblical names, *Saul* did not attract general support after the Protestant Reformation and has never been a favorite. Possibly this will change with the international reputation of novelist Saul Bellow, winner of the Nobel Prize for literature in 1976.

### Scott

Old English, "a Scotsman." Var: **Scot, Scottie, Scotty.**
A family name for centuries, it has gained acceptance

as a first name only since the early 1900s, but its popularity has grown steadily. Astronaut Scott Carpenter; figureskating champion Scott Hamilton.

## Sean

Hebrew, "God is gracious." Var: **Shane, Shaun, Shawn.**

See **John.** This Irish version of the name quickly became a favorite in the 1970s and shows no sign of going out of fashion. Actor Sean Connery.

## Sebastian

Latin, "from Sebastia." Var: **Bastian, Bastien, Sebastiano.**

An unusual name remembered primarily because of a third-century martyr whose death by arrows has been depicted in many paintings. A Spanish city is named for him. It has never been a preferred name in England or the United States, but a successful TV version of Evelyn Waugh's novel *Brideshead Revisited*, in which it is the name of a principal character, gained it wide recognition. Track champion Sebastian Coe.

## Seymour

Old French, "from St. Maur." Var: **Morey, Morrie, Morry.** See also **Murray.**

This Norman place name, the location of a medieval abbey, was introduced in England in the eleventh century. It became established as a family name, including among its bearers Jane Seymour, third wife of Henry VIII and mother of Edward VI. As a first name it wasn't introduced until the late nineteenth century; it was popular here in the early 1900s, but its popularity declined in the 1950s.

## Sidney

Old French, "from St. Denis." Var: **Sid, Syd, Sydney.**
Another place name brought to England by the Normans, with a history similar to that of *Seymour*. The contraction of a saint's name to produce a family name, frequently evolving into a first name, is not unusual—for example, the progression from St. Clair to Sinclair.

## Simon

Hebrew, "harkening." Var: **Si, Sim, Simeon.**
In addition to Simon Peter, the leader of the apostles, another disciple of Jesus was known as Simon Zelotes, and the name is linked to a number of other figures in the New Testament. It gained wide renown in England during the Middle Ages when Simon de Montfort organized a resistance to the demands of Henry III that led eventually to the first English Parliament in 1264. Even with this support, however, the name suffered a sharp decline in preference after the Protestant Reformation because of its ties to *Peter* and thus, figuratively, to the pope. Like *Peter*, it was seldom found outside rural areas, as indicated by the nursery rhyme "Simple Simon." But in the latter half of the nineteenth century, it began a recovery, and today it is finding favor with a new generation of parents.

## Stacy

Greek, "resurrection." Var: see the feminine **Anastasia.**
Both the long (*Anastasio*) and short forms of this name are occasionally used for boys, but they are more familiar in the feminine versions. Actor Stacy Keach.

### Stanley

Old English, "stony meadow." Var: **Stan, Stanleigh, Stanly.**

A familiar name in Poland as *Stanislaus*, the name of two Polish saints, it became known in England as a family name derived from a place name. Although it was in use by the early 1800s as a first name, it received worldwide attention due to the journalist and explorer Henry Stanley (whose real name was John Rowlands). His apparently casual greeting to the Scottish missionary he had sought for months in Central Africa—"Dr. Livingstone, I presume"—impressed the name on the public's imagination.

### Stephen

Greek, "crown." Var: **Etienne, Esteban, Stefan, Stefano, Stephan, Steve, Steven, Stevie.**

Stephen of Jerusalem was, as described in the New Testament, the first Christian martyr, and his story had a strong influence on the subsequent popularity of the name. It was a particular favorite in Hungary, where it was given to five kings. It appeared in England about the twelfth century, and although it showed a decline from favor in the 1600s, it has never really been out of fashion. Novelist Stephen King; baseball stars Steve Carlton, Steve Garvey; composer, musician, and singer Stevie Wonder.

### Stuart

Old English, "steward." Var: **Steward, Stewart, Stu.**

This royal name of Scotland, and of England in the seventeenth century, came originally from a title meaning "manager" or "overseer." Both *Stuart* and *Stewart* became accepted as first names in the late 1800s and are still occasionally chosen today. Actor Stuart Whitman.

— T —

## Terence

Latin, "smooth." Var: **Terencio, Terenzio, Terrance, Terrence, Terry.**

From a Roman clan name whose origin is uncertain; one possibility is given above, another is "earthly." It was the name of a writer of comic plays in the second century B.C., a former slave who took his master's name when granted his freedom. In seventeenth-century England there was a revival of interest in his work but with no apparent influence on naming; a similar family name introduced from France, Thierry, seems to have had little influence as well. It began to attract attention in the late 1800s as an export from Ireland where it had been used as an alternative to a native Irish name; by the mid-twentieth century, as *Terry*, it was a familiar name for both boys and girls.

## Theodore

Greek, "gift of God." Var: **Feodor, Ted, Tedd, Teddie, Teddy, Teodor, Teodoro, Theo.**

Although it was the name of a number of saints venerated in the Middle Ages, it was seldom found in England until the nineteenth century. This was not the case in Wales, however, which claimed its own saint by this name. It may also have been the source of the Welsh family name Tudor, the royal house that ruled England in the fifteenth and sixteenth centuries. It was seen more frequently in Europe, especially in Russia as *Feodor* (or *Fyodor*), the name of the great nineteenth-century novelist Dostoevsky (*The Brothers Karamazov*). A celebrated American novelist of the early 1900s was Theodore Dreiser, author of *An American Tragedy*. But the American who did more than anyone else to arouse interest in the name was Theodore Roosevelt, the energetic twenty-sixth president remembered for, among other things, the Panama Canal, the conservation movement, and the teddy bear.

## Thomas

Aramaic, "twin." Var: **Tam, Tammy, Tom, Tomas, Tomaso, Tommy.**

Aramaic was a common language in the Middle East during the events described in the New Testament. One of the original twelve apostles, called Judas, was given the name to distinguish him from the other apostles Jude and Judas Iscariot. It was Thomas who refused to believe in the resurrection of Jesus until he had seen the evidence with his own eyes, the basis for the expression "doubting Thomas."

The name was used in England by the twelfth century, when Thomas à Becket was Archbishop of Canterbury. A later namesake, Thomas More, was executed by Henry VIII for resisting the king's interference in church affairs. It gradually became so familiar that, like *Jack*, it was applied to a wide variety of situations and uses, ending up with two other much-employed names in the expression "Tom, Dick, and Harry," meaning everybody. In the United States Thomas Jefferson was the first secretary of state and the third president; Thomas Edison was the leading inventor of his time; and Harriet Beecher Stowe's *Uncle Tom's Cabin* and Mark Twain's *Adventures of Tom Sawyer* were two of the most popular novels of the nineteenth century.

## Timothy

Greek, "honoring God." Var: **Tim, Timmie, Timmy.**
Converted to Christianity by Paul the Apostle, Timothy was his colleague and companion on many voyages; two of the epistles or letters in the New Testament were addressed by him to Timothy. Nevertheless, the name was not often given in Europe or England until the Protestant Reformation; from that time on it has kept always on the edge of fashion without ever becoming a great favorite. Actor Timothy Bottoms.

## Tobias

Hebrew, "God is good." Var: **Tobiah, Tobin, Tobit, Toby.**
Another name revived by the Puritans that has also benefited from the recent renewal of interest in biblical names. It appears not only in the Old Testament but as one of the books (Tobit) in the Apocrypha (see **Raphael**). *Tobiah* was accepted by the Puritans as a very old name, with an attractive ring for some parents of today, but *Tobias* and *Toby* are preferred.

## Tristram

Welsh, "clamor." Var: **Tris, Tristan.**
Richard Wagner's opera *Tristan und Isolde* dramatizes the story of a knight who fell in love with a princess pledged to another and who died with her. In Arthurian legend the knight is called Tristram, an old Welsh name that may have some link to the French word *triste*, meaning "sad." Tristram Coffin won a Pulitzer Prize for poetry in 1936; Tris Speaker, member of the Baseball Hall of Fame.

## Tyrone

Irish, "land of Owen." Var: **Ty, Tye.**

The name of the county of Tyrone in Northern Ireland may be derived from a Gaelic version of the Welsh name *Owen*. Hollywood star Tyrone Power, whose career extended from the 1930s to the 1950s.

— U —

## Ulysses

Greek, "wrathful." Var: **Ulick, Ulises.**

The Latin name for a legendary Greek hero, Odysseus; several different definitions are possible, since the name in Greek has at least twelve variations. He was king of Ithaca and a leader in the war against Troy; it was his idea to build the hollow wooden horse in which the Greeks managed to enter the city. His many adventures on a ten-year voyage home are described in Homer's *Odyssey*. A very different modern account is contained in *Ulysses* (1922), by the Irish author James Joyce. Ulysses S. Grant, the eighteenth president, was commander of the Union forces in the Civil War.

## Upton

Old English, "upper town." Var: **Upten.**

A name that enjoyed some popularity around the turn of the century. In the early 1900s Upton Sinclair was a novelist and social reformer whose book about the Chicago stockyards, *The Jungle*, helped to spur food-inspection laws. He won a Pulitzer Prize for fiction in 1943.

## Uriah

Hebrew, "God is my light." Var: **Uri.**

As presented in the Second Book of Samuel, Uriah was a loyal soldier in King David's army whose death was arranged to make possible the marriage between David and Bathsheba, Uriah's wife. The biblical name was revived by the Puritans and again by the Victorians, but Charles Dickens' use of it for the unpleasant Uriah Heep in *David Copperfield* reduced its chances considerably.

## — V —

## Valentine

Latin, "strong, healthy." Var: **Val, Valentino, Valerian.**

The name of a third-century Roman martyr, it has been given in Europe and England since the Middle Ages to girls and boys, though it has served primarily as a masculine name. The practice of sending greeting cards to mark St. Valentine's Day on February 14 dates only from the last century, but the day's romantic associations are very old. It has been suggested that the day coincided with a Roman festival dedicated to Juno, which involved similar customs.

## Van

Dutch, "of, from." Var: **Vann, Vannie.**

Many old Dutch names have this prefix, but it is sometimes used as a first name in the United States. Actors Van Heflin, Van Johnson.

## Victor

Latin, "conqueror." Var: **Vic, Vittorio.**

Popular in Italy for many centuries, it has been known in other European countries since the medieval period, but it was only in the 1800s that its wider use began. The fame of Queen Victoria is generally suggested as a major reason. Victor Hugo was one of the great French authors of the nineteenth century (*Les Miserables*); Victor Herbert was a celebrated turn-of-the-century composer of operettas; Vittorio de Sica was a leading Italian film actor and director. Although the many movie versions of *Frankenstein* have made this name world-famous, it is seldom remembered that the first name of the character in Mary Shelley's novel is Victor.

## Vincent

Latin, "conquering." Var: **Vin, Vince, Vincente, Vincenzo, Vinnie, Vinny.**

Taken from the same Latin word as *Victor*, it was the name of a Spanish martyr early in the fourth century; it spread from Spain to Britain in the Middle Ages. As with many names of saints, it virtually disappeared after the Protestant Reformation; it was maintained in France by the reputation of St. Vincent de Paul in the seventeenth century, who established the Vincentian Order and the Sisters of Charity. Like *Victor*, it was adopted again in the 1800s. The Dutch artist Vincent van Gogh is one of the best-known painters of the nineteenth century.

# — W —

## Wallace

Old English, "stranger." Var: **Wallie, Wallis, Wally, Walsh.**

Even though it is English in origin, this name first became popular in Scotland, where William Wallace was a patriot and hero of the thirteenth century, preceding Robert Bruce. However, it didn't enter general use as a first name outside that country until the nineteenth century. Preference for it has declined since World War II. Wallace Beery, a movie star from the 1920s through the 1940s, won an Academy Award for *The Champ* (1931).

## Walter

Old German, "power of the army." Var: **Wallie, Wally, Walt, Wat, Watt.**

The Old English *Harold* is composed of the same basic elements but in reverse order. The name was brought to England by the Normans in the eleventh century and for several hundred years was spelled and pronounced *Wauter* (or *Water*), giving rise to the short form *Wat* and the family name Watson. By the sixteenth century *Walter* was the preferred form, and one of the best-known Elizabethans was Walter Raleigh, who sponsored early Virginia settlements and imported tobacco into England. Thus it has been known in America since the time of the first colonies, but it wasn't widely adopted until the 1800s. Walt Whitman, author of *Leaves of Grass*, was a leading American poet. The most famous bearer of the name is probably Walt Disney, creator of Mickey Mouse and Donald Duck. Football star Walter Payton; TV commentator Walter Cronkite.

## Warren

Old German, "defender." Var: **Warney.**

This Norman name also served as the basis for the title "warden," which was applied to a number of medieval posts with varying responsibilities. From it came *Ward*; a third name with a similar origin is *Warner*. After the fifteenth century all three survived primarily as family names until the Victorian period. *Warren* had a more successful return as a first name than the others. Warren Harding was the twenty-ninth president; Warren Burger, chief justice of the Supreme Court.

## Wayne

Old English, "wagon." Var: **Wain.**

A wainwright was a maker and repairer of wagons. Both elements of this occupational name eventually became family names; many centuries later both also were adopted as first names, *Wayne* being the more popular, perhaps because of actor John Wayne. Actually, "wright" was an all-purpose term for an artisan, and so it was probably considered less distinctive. Singer Wayne Newton; hockey star Wayne Gretzky.

## Wesley

Old English, "west meadow." Var: **Wes, Wesleigh, Westley.**

Like other names with this ending, it was a place name that evolved into a family name. Its adoption as a first name was aided by the reputation of John Wesley, the eighteenth-century religious reformer and founder of Methodism.

## William

Old German, "resolute guardian." Var: **Bill, Billy, Wilhelm, Will, Willi, Willie, Willis, Willy, Wilmer, Wilmot.**

The victory of William the Conqueror at Hastings in 1066 ensured that his name would have at least temporary popularity in England, but *William* has done much better than that. It was the most familiar of all masculine names until the thirteenth century, when its place was taken by *John* and *Jack*. Since then it has remained a preferred name in various forms down to the present day.

The best-known bearer of the name—perhaps the best-known Englishman—is the Elizabethan playwright and poet William Shakespeare, called Will by his friends. After the Norman conqueror, three other British kings had the name, and it has also been given to three United States presidents—the ninth (Harrison), twenty-fifth (McKinley), and twenty-seventh (Taft). The most familiar short form is *Bill*, popularized in the late nineteenth century by William Cody ("Buffalo Bill"), former frontier scout and creator of the Wild West show. *Bill* and *Billy* have also become names in their own right.

Author, columnist, and TV personality William F. Buckley; Willie Mays, member of the Baseball Hall of Fame; internationally known revivalist Billy Graham; TV journalist Bill Moyers.

## Winston

Old English, "friendly town." Var: **Win, Winnie, Winny.**

The *win-* element in this and similar names comes from an Old German word meaning "friend." Thus *Winfield* comes from "friendly field," *Winslow* from "friendly hill," and *Winthrop* from "friendly village." All share the same short forms. The most popular is *Winston*, probably because of Winston Churchill, British prime minister and national leader during World War II.

## Woodrow

Old English, "path in the woods." Var: **Wood, Woodie, Woody.**

This family name was seldom found as a first name until the election in 1912 of the twenty-eighth president, Thomas Woodrow Wilson (it was his mother's family name). He was president during World War I, and afterward tried unsuccessfully to get the United States to join the organization he had helped to create, the League of Nations, forerunner of the United Nations.

— X —

## Xavier

Arabic, "bright." Var: **Javier.**

From a Spanish place name that formed part of the name of Francis Xavier, a sixteenth-century saint who worked with Ignatius Loyola to found the Society of Jesus (Jesuits). By itself, *Xavier* (pronounced *Havier*) is usually given among Spanish-speaking families. Javier Perez de Cuellar is secretary general of the United Nations.

# — Y —

## Yves

Old French, "archer." Var: **Ives, Ivor.**

Seldom seen in English-speaking countries, *Yves* (pronounced *Eve*) is still a popular name in France. Actor and singer Yves Montand; fashion designer Yves Saint Laurent.

# — Z —

## Zachary

Hebrew, "God is renowned." Var: **Zac, Zach, Zachariah, Zacharias, Zack, Zak, Zechariah, Zeke.**

There are a number of biblical references to this name, including the Book of Zechariah, the next-to-last book of the Old Testament. In the New Testament it is the name of the father of John the Baptist. It was seldom seen in England until the Protestant Reformation, and later it was introduced in America by the Puritans. Since the 1970s it has benefited from the revival of Old Testament names. Zachary Taylor was the twelfth president.

# Bibliography: Learning
## More About Names

This is a brief listing of sources for parents who want to go further into the subject. Some of these books will be on the shelves of most bookstores, but all should be available through your local library.

Delaney, John J. *Dictionary of Saints*. New York: Doubleday & Company, Inc., 1980.
Brief biographical sketches of approximately five thousand major and minor saints (several saints usually bear the same name). The sketches include dates, birthplace, reasons for sainthood.

Dunkling, Leslie. *The Guinness Book of Names*, 2nd ed. Enfield (G.B.): Guinness Superlatives Ltd., 1983.
Chapters or sections on first names, middle names, family names, and nicknames. Lively discussion of names of other types: place names, street names, English pub names, house names, trade names, and many more.

Graves, Robert. *Greek Myths*. New York: Doubleday & Company, Inc., 1981.

An illustrated version of an earlier work. The text covers most major figures of Greek mythology, with attractive and informative color and black-and-white photos of statues, paintings, temples, etc.

Kravitz, David. *Who's Who in Greek and Roman Mythology.* New York: Clarkson N. Potter, Inc., 1975.
Brief listings that cover a wide range of mythological figures. Useful in a different way from the Graves book, which provides more extensive articles about a smaller group of figures.

Lemmons, Reuel G., et al. *The New Smith's Bible Dictionary.* New York: Doubleday & Company, Inc., 1966.
A condensed and completely revised version of a huge work that first appeared in the late nineteenth century. It offers less information about names than the McKenzie *Dictionary* but is still useful as a general source.

McKenzie, John L., S.J. *Dictionary of the Bible.* New York: Macmillan Publishing Co., 1965.
A comprehensive volume offering two thousand articles on people, places, and events in both the Old and New Testaments. Personal name entries include the language of origin and the definition.

Smith, Elsdon C. *Dictionary of American Family Names.* New York: Harper & Row, 1956.
Lists more than six thousand family names, including national origin and meaning.

Stewart, George R. *American Given Names.* New York: Oxford University Press, 1979.
Arranged in dictionary form. It provides many ex-

amples of the variety of names, naming practices, the use of family names for middle names, and discusses periodic name revivals in the United States.

Whitney, David C. *The American Presidents*. New York: Doubleday & Company, Inc., 1982.

Biographies from George Washington to Ronald Reagan. It also offers many interesting facts about presidents' wives and families, vice-presidents, cabinet members, and presidential elections.

Withycombe, E. G. *The Oxford Dictionary of English Christian Names*, 2nd ed. New York: Oxford University Press, 1971.

A standard work in its field. Makes good use of collections of names from early records, including census and tax lists, jury rosters, parish registers, etc., to establish a basis for a discussion of English naming customs.

# Index: A Complete List of Names

The names printed in *italic* are the entries in the two major name chapters. Representative variations and short forms (for example, Abbie for *Abigail*) are included in the index but not slight differences in spelling (Abby), which can be found under the principal entries in the chapters.

## Names for Girls

Alvina: Old German, "noble friend"

Amabel: see *Annabel*, 54

Amalia: see *Amelia*, 52

*Amanda*, 52

Amber: Arabic, "amber"

*Amelia*, 52

*Amy*, 53

*Anastasia*, 53

*Andrea*, 53

*Angela*, 53

Angelique: see *Angela*, 53

Anita: see *Anne*, 54

*Annabel*, 54

*Anne*, 54

Annemarie: see *Anne*, 54, *Mary*, 99

Annick: see *Anne*, 54

*Antonia*, 55

Antoinette: see *Antonia*, 55

*April*, 55

Arabella: see *Annabel*, 54

Ardelle: Latin, "zealous"

Aretha: Greek, "virtue"

Arielle: Hebrew, "lion of God"

*Arlene*, 55

*Ashley*, 55

Astrid: Scandinavian, "God strength"

*Audrey*, 56

Augusta: Latin, "sacred"

Aurelia: Latin, "golden"

Aurora: Latin, "dawn"

Ava: see *Eve*, 72

Avery: see *Avery* (m.), 136

Avis: see Hedwig

Babette: see *Barbara*, 56

Bambi: Italian, "child"

*Barbara*, 56

Barrie: see *Barry*, 137

*Beatrice*, 57

Becky: see *Rebecca*, 112

*Belinda*, 57

Bella: Italian, "beautiful"

Belle: French, "beautiful"

Benita: Spanish, "blessed"

Bernadette: see *Bernard*, 138

Bernice: Greek, "bringer of victory"

Bertha: Old German, "bright"

Beryl: Greek, "beryl stone"

Bess: see *Elizabeth*, 69

*Beth*, 57

Betsy: see *Elizabeth*, 69

Betty: see *Elizabeth*, 69

Beulah: Hebrew, "married"

*Beverly*, 57

*Bianca*, 58

Billie: see *Wilhelmina*, 125

Blanche: see *Bianca*, 58

Blythe: Old English, "happy"

Bobbie: see *Barbara*, 56, *Robert*, 197

Bonita: see *Bonnie*, 58

*Bonnie*, 58

Brenda: see *Brendan*, 139

Brett: see *Brett* (m.), 139

*Bridget*, 58

Brigitte: see *Bridget*, 58

*Brooke*, 59

Caitlin: see *Catherine*, 61

*Camilla*, 59

*Candace*, 59

*Daisy,* 65
Dale: see *Dale* (m.), 148
Damita: Latin, "little doe"
*Dana,* 65
*Danielle,* 65
Daphne: see *Laura,* 92
Daria: Greek, "wealthy"
Darlene: Old English, "darling"
Davida: see *David,* 150
*Dawn,* 65
*Deborah,* 66
*Deirdre,* 66
Delia: see *Diana,* 66
Delilah: Hebrew, "delight"
Della: see *Adeline,* 50
Dena: Old English, "from the valley"
Denise: see *Dennis,* 150
*Diana,* 66
Dina: see Dena
Dinah: Hebrew, "judged"
Dixie: the American South (originally slang for New Orleans)
Dodie: see *Dorothy,* 68
Dolly: see *Dolores,* 67, *Dorothy,* 68
*Dolores,* 67
Dominique: see *Dominic,* 151
*Donna,* 67
Dora: see *Dorothy,* 68
Doreen: Irish, probably from Dora
Dory: see *Doris,* 67
*Doris,* 67
*Dorothy,* 68
Dotty: see *Dorothy,* 68
Dulcie: Latin, "sweetness"

Eartha: Old German, "of the earth"
Edie: see *Edith,* 68
*Edith,* 68
*Edna,* 68
Edwina: see *Edwin,* 154
Effie: see Euphemia
*Eileen,* 69
*Elaine,* 69
*Eleanor,* 69
Elise: see *Elizabeth,* 69
Eliza: see *Elizabeth,* 69
*Elizabeth,* 69
Ella: Old German, "all"
Ellen: see *Elaine,* 69
Eloise: see *Louise,* 95
Elsa: see *Elizabeth,* 69
*Emily,* 70
*Emma,* 70
Enid: Welsh, "soul"
*Erica,* 71
*Erin,* 71
Ernestine: see *Ernest,* 157
*Estelle,* 71
*Esther,* 72
*Ethel,* 72
Etta: see *Harriet,* 79
Eugenia: see *Eugene,* 157
Eunice: Greek, "happy victory"
Euphemia: Greek, "pleasant speech"
Evangeline: see *Eve,* 72
*Eve,* 72
*Evelyn,* 73

Fabia: Latin, "bean-grower"
*Faith,* 73
Fanchon: see *Frances,* 75

*Harriet,* 79
Hattie: see *Harriet,* 79
*Hayley,* 80
Hazel: Old English,
  "hazelnut tree"
*Heather,* 80
Hedda: see Hedwig
Hedwig: Old German,
  "refuge in war"
Heidi: see *Adeline,* 50
*Helen,* 80
Helga: Scandinavian,
  "holy"
Heloise: see *Louise,* 95
Henrietta: see *Harriet,* 79
Hermione: Greek, "of the
  world"
Hester: see *Esther,* 72
*Hilary,* 81
Hilda: Old German, "battle
  maid"
Hildegarde: Old German,
  "battle spear"
*Hollis,* 81
*Honor,* 81
*Hope,* 82
Hortense: Latin, "of a
  garden"
Hyacinth: Greek, "hyacinth
  plant"

Ida: Old German, "hard-
  working"
Ilona: see *Helen,* 80
Ilsa: see Elsa
Imogene: possibly Latin,
  "image"
Ina: derived from names
  with this ending, such as
  Carolina

Inez: see *Agnes,* 51
Inga: see *Ingrid,* 82
*Irene,* 82
*Iris,* 83
Irma: Old German,
  "universal"
*Isabel,* 83
Isadora: Greek, "gift of
  Isis"
Isolde: Welsh, "fair one"
*Ivy,* 83

Jacinda: see Hyacinth
Jackie: see *Jacqueline,* 83
*Jacqueline,* 83
Jaime: see *Jamie,* 84
*Jamie,* 84
*Jane,* 84
Janine: see *Jane,* 84
Janis: see *Jane,* 84
*Jasmin,* 85
*Jean,* 85
Jemima: Hebrew, "dove"
*Jennifer,* 85
Jeri: see *Geraldine,* 77
Jesse: see *Jesse* (m.), 175
*Jessica,* 86
Jill: see *Gillian,* 77
Jo: short form of names
  with this beginning,
  such as *Joanne,* 86
*Joan,* 86
*Joanne,* 86
*Jocelyn,* 87
*Jodie,* 87
*Joelle,* 87
Jolie: French, "pretty"
Josephine: see *Joseph,* 177
Josie: see Josephine
*Joy,* 88

Lulu: see *Louise*, 95

Lydia: Greek, "from Lydia"

Lynn: see *Linda*, 94 (see also Linette)

Mabel: see *Annabel*, 54

*Madeline*, 96

Madge: see *Margaret*, 97

Magda: see *Madeline*, 96

Maggie: see *Margaret*, 97

Mahalia: Hebrew, "affection"

Mady: see *Madeline*, 96

Maisie: see *Margaret*, 97

Mame: see *Mary*, 99

Mandy: see *Amanda*, 52

Mara: see *Mary*, 99

Marcella: see *Marcia*, 97

*Marcia*, 97

*Margaret*, 97

Margery: see *Margaret*, 97

Margie: see *Margaret*, 97

Margot: see *Margaret*, 97

Marguerite: see *Margaret*, 97

Maria: see *Mary*, 99

*Marianne*, 98

Maribel: see *Mary*, 99; Belle

Marietta: see *Mary*, 99

Marilyn: see *Marlene*, 98

Marina: Latin, "of the sea"

*Marlene*, 98

Marnie: see Marina

Marsha: see *Marcia*, 97

Marta: see *Martha*, 99

*Martha*, 99

Martita: see *Martha*, 99

*Mary*, 99

Marylou: see *Mary*, 99; *Louise*, 95

Matilda: Old German, "battle strength"

Maude: see Matilda

Maura: see *Maureen*, 100

*Maureen*, 100

Mavis: French, "thrush"

Maxine: Latin, "greatest"

*May*, 100

Meg: see *Megan*, 100

*Megan*, 100

*Melanie*, 101

Melesina: see *Millicent*, 103

*Melinda*, 101

Melisande: see *Millicent*, 103

*Melissa*, 101

Melody: Greek, "choral song"

Mercedes: Spanish, "mercies"

Meredith: Welsh, "great chief"

*Merle*, 102

Mia: see *Mary*, 99

*Michelle*, 102

Mignon: French, "cute"

*Mildred*, 102

*Millicent*, 103

Millie: short form of names with this beginning (*Mildred*, 102) or ending (*Emily*, 70)

Mimi: see *Mary*, 99

Mina: see *Wilhelmina*, 125

Minnie: see *Mary*, 99; *Wilhelmina*, 125

Mira: see *Miranda*, 103
*Miranda,* 103
*Miriam,* 103
Mitzi: see *Miriam*, 103
Moira: see *Maureen*, 100
*Molly,* 103
Mona: Irish, "noble"
Monica: possibly Latin, "adviser"
Morgana: Welsh, "great and fair"
*Muriel,* 104
Myrna: Irish, "beloved"
Myrtle: Greek, "myrtle plant"

Nadia: see *Nadine*, 104
*Nadine,* 104
Nan: see *Nancy*, 104
*Nancy,* 104
*Naomi,* 105
*Natalie,* 105
Natasha, see *Natalie*, 105
Nedda: feminine form of Ned (see *Edward*, 154)
Nelia: see Cornelia
Nell: see *Eleanor*, 69
Nerissa: Latin, "sea nymph"
Nessa: see *Agnes*, 51
Netty: short form of names with this ending, such as Janette
*Nicole,* 105
*Nina,* 106
Nita: short form of names with this ending, such as Juanita
Noelle: see *Natalie*, 105

Nola: an Italian place name
Nora: see *Eleanor*, 69
Noreen: Irish, probably from Nora
*Norma,* 106
Nydia: Latin, "from the nest"

Octavia: Latin, "eighth"
Odelia: see *Odetta*, 106
*Odetta,* 106
Olga: see Helga
*Olivia,* 107
Olympia: Greek, "heavenly"
Ona: see *Una*, 122
Ondine: Latin, "little wave" (a water spirit)
Oona: see *Una*, 122
Opal: Sanskrit, "precious stone"
Ophelia: Greek, "help"
Oriana: Latin, "dawning"
Ottilie: see *Odetta*, 106

Paloma: Spanish, "dove"
*Pamela,* 107
Pandora: Greek, "all gifts"
Patience: Latin, "forbearance"
*Patricia,* 108
Patty: see *Patricia*, 108
*Paula,* 108
*Pearl,* 108
Peggy: see *Margaret*, 97
*Penelope,* 109
Penny: see *Penelope*, 109
Pepita: Spanish, a short form of Josephine

Perdita: Latin, "lost"

Peta: see Petra

Petra: see *Peter*, 192

*Petula*, 109

Petunia: Tupi Indian, "petunia plant"

Philippa: see *Philip*, 193

Philomena: Greek, "nightingale"

Phoebe: Greek, "shining one"

*Phyllis*, 109

Pia: Latin, "pious"

Pier: Old French form of *Peter*, 192

Pilar: Spanish, "pillar"

*Polly*, 110

Pollyanna: see *Polly*, 110

Poppy: Old English, "poppy plant"

Portia: Latin, from a clan name originally meaning "swineherd"

*Priscilla*, 110

*Prudence*, 110

Prunella: Latin, "little plum"

*Queena*, 111

*Quentin*, 111

Queta: see *Quentin*, 111

Quita: see *Quentin*, 111

*Rachel*, 111

Ramona: see *Raymond*, 195

Raquel: see *Rachel*, 111

Reba: see *Rebecca*, 112

*Rebecca*, 112

*Regan*, 112

Regina: see *Queena*, 111; *Regan*, 112

Renata: Latin, "reborn"

Rene: see *Irene*, 82

Rhea: Greek, an earth goddess

Rhoda: see *Rose*, 113

Rita: see *Margaret*, 97

Roberta: see *Robert*, 197; *Robin*, 112

*Robin*, 112

*Rochelle*, 113

Rona: see Rowena

Rosalie: see *Rose*, 113

*Rosalind*, 113

Rosamond: Latin, "pure rose"

*Rose*, 113

*Rosemary*, 114

Rowena: Welsh, "slender and fair"

Roxane: Persian, "dawn"

Ruby: Latin, "red stone"

*Ruth*, 114

Sabina: Latin, "woman of the Sabines" (an ancient Italian tribe)

Sabrina: Latin, a water spirit (from the Severn River in Britain)

Sadie: see *Sarah*, 116

*Sally*, 115

Salome: Hebrew, "peaceful"

*Samantha*, 115

Samara: Hebrew, "kept by God"

Sandra: see *Alexandra*, 51

Trixie: see *Beatrice*, 57
*Trudy*, 122

Ulrica: Old German, "wolf rule"
Undine: see Ondine
*Una*, 122
Unity: Latin, "one"
*Ursula*, 122
Uta: see *Odetta*, 106

Val: short form of names with this beginning, such as *Valerie*, 123
Valentina: see *Valentine*, 209
*Valerie*, 123
*Vanessa*, 123
Velma: see *Wilhelmina*, 125
Venetia: possibly a Latin form of Gwyneth (may also be from Venice)
*Vera*, 123
Verna: Latin, "springlike"
*Veronica*, 124
Vickie: see *Victoria*, 124
*Victoria*, 124
Vida: see Davida
Viola: see *Violet*, 124
*Violet*, 124
*Virginia*, 125
Vita: Latin, "life" (may also be a variation of Vida)
Vivian: Latin, "alive"

*Wanda*, 125
Wendy: see *Gwendolen*, 78
*Wilhelmina*, 125

Willa: see *Wilhelmina*, 125
Wilma: see *Wilhelmina*, 125
*Winifred*, 126
Winnie: see *Winifred*, 126
Winona: American Indian, "firstborn"
Wynne: see Gwyneth

Xanthe: Greek, "yellow"
*Xaviera*, 126
Xenia: Greek, "guest"

Yasmin: see *Jasmin*, 85
Yetta: possibly a form of Henrietta
*Yolanda*, 126
Yvette: see *Yvonne*, 127
*Yvonne*, 127

Zandra: see Sandra
*Zelda*, 127
Zenia: see Xenia
Zenobia: possibly from a Greek form meaning "life from Zeus"
Zia: Italian, "aunt"
Zipporah: Hebrew, "bird"
Zita: short form of names with this ending, such as Rosita
*Zoe*, 127
Zora: Arabic, "dawn"

## Names for Boys

*Aaron*, 129
Abba: Hebrew, "father"

Barton: Old English,
"barley town"

Basil: Greek, "kingly"

Baxter: Old English,
"baker"

Bayard: Old French,
"reddish brown"

Beau: see Beauregard

Beauregard: Old French,
"good-looking"

Benedict: Latin, "blessed"

*Benjamin*, 137

Berkeley: see Barclay

*Bernard*, 138

Bert: short form of names
with this beginning
(Bertram) or ending
(*Albert*, 131)

Bertram: Old German,
"bright raven"

Bill: see *William*, 213

Blair: Scottish, "marshy
plain"

Blake: Old English, "dark"

Bob: see *Robert*, 197

Boris: Russian, "fight"

Boyd: Scottish, "fair-
haired"

*Bradford*, 139

Bradley: see *Bradford*, 139

Bram: see *Abraham*, 130

Brandon: see *Brendan*, 139

*Brendan*, 139

Brent: Old English, "steep
hill"

*Brett*, 139

*Brian*, 140

*Broderick*, 140

Brook: see *Brooke*, 59

*Bruce*, 140

Bruno: Old German,
"brown"

Bryant: see *Brian*, 140

Burgess: Old German,
"town dweller"

Burl: Old English,
probably a short form of
Burleigh, "town
meadow"

*Burton*, 141

*Byron*, 141


Caleb: Hebrew, "dog"
(implying affection and
loyalty)

*Calvin*, 142

Cameron: Scottish,
"crooked nose"

*Carey*, 142

*Carl*, 142

Carleton: see *Charlton*,
144

Carroll: see *Carl*, 142

*Casey*, 143

Casper: Persian, "keeper of
the treasure."

Cecil: see *Cecilia*, 61

Cedric: probably Old
English, "amiable"

*Charles*, 143

*Charlton*, 144

Chester: Old English,
"fortified camp"

*Christian*, 144

*Christopher*, 145

Chuck: see *Charles*, 143

Clare: see *Clare* (f.), 62

Clarence: Latin, "famous"
(a variation of the basic
meaning, "bright")

meaning "great or round hill"

Graham: an English place name, meaning uncertain

*Grant,* 164

Grantland: see *Grant,* 164

Grantley: see *Grant,* 164

*Gregory,* 164

Griffith: Welsh, "strong warrior"

Grover: Old English, "grove dweller"

Gunther: Old German, "bold in battle"

Gus: see Augustus, Gustave

Gustave: Old German, possibly "noble staff"

Guy: Old German, possibly "wood" or "wide" (also associated with a Latin word meaning "lively")

Hal: see *Harold,* 165; *Henry,* 166

Hamilton: a place name in Scotland, possibly "castle town"

Hank: see *Henry,* 166

Hans: see *John,* 176

Harlan: Old German, "army land"

*Harold,* 165

Harper: Old English, "harp player"

Harry: see *Harold,* 165; *Henry,* 166

Hartley: Old English,

"stone meadow"

*Harvey,* 166

Hector: Greek, "steadfast"

Hedley: Old English, "grassy meadow"

*Henry,* 166

*Herbert,* 167

*Herman,* 167

Hershel: Old German, "little deer"

Hilary: see *Hilary* (f.), 81

Hilliard: Old German, "battle brave"

Hiram: Hebrew, "exalted"

Hobart: see Hubert

Hollis: see *Hollis* (f.), 81

Homer: Greek, "pledge"

*Horace,* 167

Hosea: Hebrew, "salvation" (related to *Joshua,* 178)

*Howard,* 168

Hubert: Old German, "bright mind"

*Hugh,* 168

Hugo: see *Hugh,* 168

Humphrey: Old German, meaning uncertain (possibly "great peace")

Hyman: Hebrew, "life"

*Ian,* 169

Ignatius: Latin, "fiery"

Ingemar: Scandinavian, "famous son"

*Ira,* 169

*Irving,* 169

Irwin: see *Irving,* 169

*Isaac,* 169

Isidore: Greek, "gift of
    Isis"
Israel: Hebrew, "ruling
    with God"
*Ivan*, 170

*Jack*, 170
*Jacob*, 171
Jacques: see *James*, 172
Jaime: see *James*, 172
Jake: see *Jacob*, 171
*James*, 172
Jamie: see *James*, 172;
    *Jamie* (f.), 84
Jan: see *John*, 176
*Jason*, 173
Jasper: see Casper
Jay: Old French,
    "chatterer" (also a short
    form of names with this
    beginning)
Jean: see *John*, 176
Jedidiah: Hebrew, "beloved
    of God"
Jeff: short form of
    Jefferson, *Jeffrey*, 173
Jefferson: Old English,
    "son of Jeffrey"
*Jeffrey*, 173
Jeremiah: see *Jeremy*, 174
*Jeremy*, 174
*Jerome*, 174
Jerry: short form of names
    beginning *Ger-* and *Jer-*
*Jesse*, 175
Jim, Jimmy: see *James*,
    172
Jock: see *Jack*, 170
*Jody*, 175
Joe: see *Joseph*, 177

*Joel*, 175
*John*, 176
Jon: see *John*, 176;
    *Jonathan*, 177
*Jonah*, 176
*Jonathan*, 177
Jordan: Hebrew,
    "descending"
Jose: see *Joseph*, 177
*Joseph*, 177
*Joshua*, 178
Josiah: Hebrew, "God
    heals"
Juan: see *John*, 176
Judah: Hebrew, "praised"
Jude: see Judah
Jules: see *Julian*, 178
*Julian*, 178
Julius: see *Julian*, 178
Justin: Latin, "just"

Karl: see *Carl*, 142
Keefe: Irish, "loved"
Keenan: Old English,
    "sharp" (or possibly
    Irish, "small and wise")
*Keith*, 178
Kelly: see *Kelly* (f.), 91
Kelvin: Scottish, "from the
    narrow river"
Ken: short form of names
    with this beginning,
    such as Kendall
Kendall: Scottish, "from
    the bright valley"
Kendrick: Old English,
    "valiant ruler"
*Kenneth*, 179
*Kent*, 179
Kermit: Irish, "free man"

Manfred: Old German, "man of peace"

Manuel: short form of Emmanuel

Marcel: see *Mark*, 184

Marcus: see *Mark*, 184

Mario: Italian, masculine form of *Mary*, 99

*Mark*, 184

Marlon: see Merlin

Marshall: Old German, "keeper of horses"

*Martin*, 185

Marvin: Old English, "famous friend" (may also be a form of Merlin)

*Matthew*, 185

Maurice: Latin, "Moor" (see also *Murray*, 187)

Max: see Maximilian

Maximilian: Latin, "greatest"

Maxwell: Old English, "large spring"

Maynard: Old German, "strong courage"

Melville: a French place name (Malleville)

*Melvin*, 186

Meredith: Welsh, "great chief"

Merle: see *Merle* (f.), 102

Merlin: Welsh, "sea hill" (a merlin is also a type of hawk)

Merrill: see Merle

Mervin: see Marvin

*Michael*, 186

Miles: possibly Old German, "beloved" (also an early form of *Michael*, 186, in England, and may be related to an ancient term for the Irish)

Millard: Old English, "mill-keeper"

*Milton*, 186

Mischa: see *Michael*, 186

Mitchell: see *Michael*, 186

Mohammed: Arabic, "praiseworthy"

Montgomery: a county in Wales, probably from a French place name (Mont Goumeril)

Monty: see Montgomery

Morey: see Maurice

Mortimer: a French place name (Mortemer)

*Moses*, 187

Moss: see *Moses*, 187

*Murray*, 187

Myron: Greek, "fragrant"

Nathan: see *Nathaniel*, 187

*Nathaniel*, 187

Ned: see *Edward*, 154

Nehemiah: Hebrew, "consolation of God"

*Neil*, 188

Nelson: Old English, "son of Neil"

Nestor: Greek, "traveler" (figuratively, a wise old man)

Neville: a French place name (Neuville)

Newell: see Noel

Prescott: Old English, "priest's cottage"

Preston: Old English, "priest's town"

Primo: Latin, "first, firstborn"

*Quentin*, 193

*Quincy*, 194

*Quinn*, 194

Radcliffe: Old English, "red cliff"

Rafe: see *Raphael*, 195

*Ralph*, 194

Ramon: see *Raymond*, 195

Ramsey: Old English, "ram's island"

Randall: see *Randolph*, 195

*Randolph*, 195

Raoul: see *Ralph*, 194

*Raphael*, 195

*Raymond*, 195

Regan: see *Regan* (f.), 112

*Reginald*, 196

Reid: Old English, "red"

Reuben: Hebrew, "behold, a son" (or possibly "renewer")

*Rex*, 196

Reynard: Old German, "great courage" (figuratively, a fox, from medieval tales)

Rhett: a family name, possibly Welsh, used as a first name by Margaret Mitchell in *Gone With the Wind*

Rhys: Welsh, "rashness"

*Richard*, 197

Rick: see *Richard*, 197

*Robert*, 197

Robin: see *Robin* (f.), 112 (see also *Robert*, 197)

Rockwell: Old English, "rocky spring"

*Roderick*, 198

Rodney: Old English, "reed island"

*Roger*, 198

Roland: Old German, "famous land"

*Ronald*, 199

Rory: see *Roderick*, 198

Roscoe: Old German, "deer forest"

Ross: Old French, "red" (see also *Russell*, 200)

*Roy*, 199

Rudolph: Old German, "famous wolf" (see also *Ralph*, 194)

Rufus: Latin, "red, reddish"

Rupert: see *Robert*, 197

*Russell*, 200

*Ryan*, 200

Salvatore: Latin, "savior"

Samson: Hebrew, "sunlike"

*Samuel*, 200

Sanford: Old English, "sandy river-crossing"

*Saul*, 201

Schuyler: Dutch, "giving shelter"

*Scott*, 201

Seamus: see *James*, 172

# About the Author

Martin Kelly has written many articles and stories for national magazines. The history of naming is one of his long-time interests. He created and produced a wide range of educational materials for leading health-care agencies.

# BRINGING UP BABY

A series of practical baby care and family living guides developed with the staff of *PARENTS™ MAGAZINE*. Explains both the whys and how-to's of infant care.